PRAISE FOR *KIDS CAN*

Once again, Andrew's pulse on the educational landscape results in a message that is timely and spot-on for teachers needing insight into how to move forward in supporting their students. His practical advice and strategies in *Kids Can* can be implemented by any teacher who has a desire to see their students succeed.

—**Michelle Swain,** director of gifted and advanced academic services, Round Rock ISD, TX

Andrew Sharos has significantly influenced our approach by championing the belief that "all kids can" succeed when given the right support and encouragement. His guidance has been pivotal in implementing our "AP for All" program, empowering students who might never have considered AP courses to embrace these opportunities and thrive.

—**Christina Smith,** statistics teacher and AP advisor, Kingsway Regional High School, NJ

Kids Can is exactly what I needed, and the timing of it is perfect. Educators are overwhelmed every day, and we often forget to stop and reflect on the importance of building relationships. For decades, teachers have been the pillars of trust and guidance for struggling students, but in today's classrooms, we are all struggling. Sharos mentions that "Struggling students need us more than ever." I think struggling teachers need this book more than ever. Sharos offers practical solutions.

—**Andres Ayala,** social studies coordinator, South Texas ISD, TX

Kids Can provides a valuable look into the challenges facing struggling students and offers practical solutions for educators. The focus on classroom culture and the importance of teacher belief makes this a must-read for anyone interested in improving student success.

—**Albert Hetrick,** principal, Aliamanu Middle School, Honolulu, HI

Kids Can is a must-read for educators! Drawing from his firsthand classroom experience, Sharos truly understands what drives student engagement and shares practical, impactful strategies for motivation and skill-building. Having worked with Andrew in my district, I've seen firsthand how his insights empower teachers to make small yet powerful changes that lead to significant gains in student achievement. This book is an invaluable resource for any teacher looking to inspire, motivate, and make a lasting difference in the classroom!

—**Jill Hackney,** director of advanced academics, Northside ISD, San Antonio, TX

Andrew Sharos's unwavering belief that ALL students can achieve success is contagious. Once again, *Kids Can* proves that relationships, rigor, relevance, and the right mindset are powerful tools when impacting students' social/emotional growth and academic excellence. Achieving begins with believing!

—**Ginny Nolen,** curriculum coordinator, Bossier Parish, LA

Andrew has delivered outstanding professional development for teachers at my school. His deep compassion for supporting educators is evident in this book, as his focus is not just on the high achievers but the students who struggle the most. His unwavering patience and commitment to seeing initiatives through have been instrumental in ensuring more students have the opportunity to excel. I am forever grateful for the learning experiences.

—**Dr. Porsha Denson,** assistant principal, South Gwinnett High School, GA

Kids Can

Kids CAN

Transform the Lives
of Struggling Students through
Culture, Motivation, and Methods

ANDREW SHAROS

Kids Can: Transform the Lives of Struggling Students through Culture, Motivation, and Methods
© 2025 Andrew Sharos

All rights reserved. No part of this publication may be reproduced in any form or by any electronic or mechanical means, including information storage and retrieval systems, without permission in writing by the publisher, except by a reviewer who may quote brief passages in a review. For information regarding permission, contact the publisher at books@daveburgessconsulting.com.

> This book is available at special discounts when purchased in quantity for educational purposes or for use as premiums, promotions, or fundraisers. For inquiries and details, contact the publisher at books@daveburgessconsulting.com.

Published by Dave Burgess Consulting, Inc.
Vancouver, WA
DaveBurgessConsulting.com

Library of Congress Control Number: 2025936690
Paperback ISBN: 978-1-956306-93-4
Ebook ISBN: 978-1-956306-94-1

Cover and interior design by Liz Schreiter
Edited and produced by Reading List Editorial
ReadingListEditorial.com

For my boys.

CONTENTS

Foreword by Brian Wojtun 1
Introduction 5
Chapter 1: Building Culture 14
Chapter 2: Motivation 38
Chapter 3: Attacking Skill Deficiency 51
Chapter 4: Be the Difference 74
Chapter 5: Assessment, Homework, and the Use of Data 98
Epilogue 120
Book Study Cheat Sheet 122
Book Study Questions 126

Acknowledgments 129
About the Author 131
Endnotes 133
More from Dave Burgess Consulting, Inc. 136

FOREWORD
Brian Wojtun

When Andrew asked me, his former teacher and coach, to write the foreword for his third book, I reacted just like many of our students would. I asked Google, "How do I write a foreword?" The first search query said, "Explain why you were asked to write the foreword."

I found myself at a loss for words, still wondering why he chose me. Then I read the book and realized that I was the kind of kid Andrew is trying to help.

Like many of our students, my life's journey to be able to write this today has been anything but easy. As a child, my mother continually used alcohol to resolve problems and never had enough time for me or my sister. I was blessed to have a hardworking father who did everything he could to give us the best life but struggled to make ends meet. I remember sleeping on a king-sized bed (that doubled as a couch) with my dad and sister. Academically, I struggled with dyslexia. I was the student in the back of the class trying to become invisible, feeling like my challenges were all bigger than me. A decade ago, I was diagnosed with a brain tumor that couldn't fully be removed. Despite three surgeries and the best doctors, I still carry my "ornament" with me daily. Whether they be personal, academic, or emotional challenges, I am not unlike the students Andrew describes in this book. We all know there are reasons why students act in certain ways. The challenge lies in understanding why.

The good news is, *Kids Can* will give you hope and confidence that you are not alone in the journey. It's an incredibly personal book; the situations he describes with students who struggle are very real for all of us. His solutions are both logical and empathetic. Whether you are taking the first steps of your educational journey or you are a traveled veteran, *Kids Can* will give you innovative and engaging perspectives to help motivate students, develop culture, and build the foundation for a successful classroom. There is a process, and we must trust the students to be a part of it.

During my first year teaching, I remember forming a relationship with a student who openly told me she hated history. I made it my goal to give her a better experience in my class. As we built trust, she told me all about her challenges and the grief she experienced with the death of her nana. At the end of the year, she gave me a redheaded troll with a blue and white shirt. I remember thinking, "I am twenty-two years old, what am I going to do with a troll?" She told me it was a gift from Nana, and she wanted me to have it. My reaction went from "A troll?" to "A TROLL!" I was so excited as the troll took center stage on my desk. Each year, I tell my classes this story, and after thirty-one years, there are 150 trolls around my room, each with their own story to tell. Culture and relationships matter.

During my career, I've tried to model the same vulnerabilities that our students must feel. At the beginning of the year, I show them slides called "The Journey of Life." The presentation highlights the fun times as well as the many challenges I've faced. I allow the students the opportunity to ask me any questions they are curious about. Then, it's the students' turn. They construct a slide deck of their lives where I learn about them. In this book, Andrew encourages you to break down these walls in order to build relationships with each individual student and the class as a whole.

It is in this vein that I share this foreword with you today. I've been blessed to build so many great relationships with students over the years.

One such relationship is with the author of this book.

I remember the six-foot-four, 155-pound pitcher who couldn't break a pane of glass with his fastball but could hit a fly on a wall from sixty feet away. He wanted the ball in his hands in every big situation. One of the qualities I admire most about Andrew is his resiliency. He refused to quit, never saying, "I can't do it" but wanting to prove that he could. It's the main reason he excelled as a player and now excels as an educator. When all of his students received passing scores on the AP exam and set school and state records along the way, I was not surprised. Kids can . . . when led by a teacher who believes it to be true.

Over the years, I have been fortunate to become closer to Andrew and his family. Now I attend his son's baseball games. It is surreal to think, *I coached their dad*—certainly a "how time flies by" moment. Last year, I remember his son running with a glove in between innings. I was excited to watch him pitch, just like I'd seen his father do countless times before. But, instead of running to the bullpen to warm up, he ran toward me and asked, "Coach, could you please play catch with me before I go in?"

Andrew knew I was a catcher as a player, and to have his son ask me to help him really moved me. As we began to play catch, something happened that I did not expect. Tears started to run down my face. My entire life began passing me by—the struggles of my childhood and the years of trying to figure out who I was as a student, teacher, and person.

It finally clicked. My tears of sorrow turned to joy, knowing all the hard work was vindicated in this one brief moment in time. In the end, isn't that what we all want? To know that the journey was worth it? Our relationship was recursive, now being built with the next generation.

We want to make a difference in our students' lives. *Kids Can* will encourage you to be the difference. If only I had this book earlier in my career, it would have expedited my learning curve and given me a better perspective of what education is all about.

Our relationship has blossomed into a mutual respect, a shared love of teaching, and a cherished friendship. Despite the fact that I am a decade older than Andrew, this book has had a profound effect on me, and his words are beyond his years. It helps, too, that he has collected thoughts and stories from teachers around the country to build agency with us readers. He gives us countless strategies for helping students learn how to read, write, and think—suggestions you can use tomorrow in class.

Each of us has an opportunity to move students toward success, knowing it will be worth it in the end. Your journey will be challenging, yet altogether possible. Luckily for us, now we have this resource that can help us toward the final destination, building a classroom culture that motivates, inspires, and supports our struggling students in reaching the ultimate goal—their full potential.

INTRODUCTION

It was Black Friday, the day following Thanksgiving. Amid the hustle and bustle of shopping and the start of the holiday season, my wife sent me to the basement to bring up the Christmas decorations. Frequently, when I dust off something from the storage room, I end up distracted by what I find and spend more time on my discovery than the task at hand. On this day, I stumbled upon a beat-up green folder, frayed at each corner.

I opened it and began combing through its contents. The folder contained many documents I'd needed to apply for my teaching license, some letters of recommendation, and a very thin résumé. I remember all of these documents; it was the "prepare for my first interview" folder.

In the very back of this old folder, I found a letter. It was addressed to the parents of the 2004 Wheatland Ducks, a travel baseball team I'd coached as my summer job in college. The letter outlined the expectations for the players, including rules and goals we shared for the season. Email was relatively new at the time, and I am guessing I sent physical letters containing these rules to the parents, hoping they would relay them to the kids.

I reminisced as I read the letter, thinking about the players and the amazing memories we shared. I laughed at a few of the things I'd written; hindsight is always 20/20. I snapped a few pictures of the letter and texted it to former players and my assistant coaches. I found myself firmly down a nostalgic rabbit hole, while only moments from facing the wrath of the Christmas countdown. All was not lost, however, as I did finally decide on the theme of this book.

This book is long overdue. In fact, there might be an argument that this book should have been written before its predecessor. When I wrote *All 4s and 5s: A Guide to Teaching and Leading Advanced Placement Programs* several years ago, I'd been motivated to share the soulful story of a group of underdog students who achieved the best test scores in the nation. The ultimate goal of the book was to help teachers achieve similar results in their different contexts. But there was something missing.

For starters, by connecting the book to the AP and College Board community, I'd focused on an audience of mostly AP teachers. Interestingly enough, the feedback from people who read the book suggested the scope was quite a bit broader. (And at the time this current book is published, there are some fifteen thousand copies of my previous book out there.) Most folks seemed to find that the book was not about teaching AP students and leading AP programs, but rather about good teaching. Within and beyond the AP community, it has been as a guide to impactful instructional practices and culture-building within a cohort of students.

The book has taken on a life of its own. Entire faculties have read the book to learn how to design instructional practices that focus on high standards and expectations. But feedback has told me there was something missing. As I've traveled to different schools and speaking engagements across the country, I've encountered some of the same themes and questions from audiences:

- "My classes are populated with many students who lack the skills and content knowledge to be academically successful in a difficult class."
- "The apathy toward homework and completing anything outside of school is real."

- "Open enrollment has doubled the number of students enrolling in advanced classes in our school."
- "When students cannot access and read the text within the discipline, how can I help them?"
- "I cannot create classroom culture when my class rosters seem to change daily, and our student population is extremely transient."
- "I don't receive the support from students' parents like I used to."
- "My students lack the motivation to complete challenging academic work, and I feel like I am constantly fighting for their attention."
- "How can I advance students' skills when they are so behind on content from the previous classes?"
- "The variance in ability level of my students makes it too hard to effectively differentiate."
- "My students cheat on their work and specifically their writing. AI is hurting my ability to assess student progress."
- "Our school community, specifically our parents and students, do not value attendance anymore."

Perhaps more broadly stated, teachers wanted to know, "What can I do to help students who are struggling academically and personally?"

Clearly, something was missing.

Our struggling students need us, and hopefully by reading this book, you will feel less alone in this challenge. In the past, I've found pride and a sense of accomplishment in celebrating our students' test scores. This book will make little mention of test scores. While celebrating a measurable data point can validate our work as educators, helping students who struggle is a larger calling for all of us.

So if we aren't celebrating a measurable data point, what data should we focus on?

The No Child Left Behind Act of 2001 sort of drove this bus by focusing first on Title I schools and lower-performing populations. Schools have adapted to highlight different data. High schools boast the number of students in career and technical education programs. Our students graduate ready for the workforce with certifications, job skills, and confidence to enter a new field. Elementary and secondary schools focus more on growth.

We cannot always change where students start, but we can certainly affect where they finish. Working with struggling students specifically provides the most satisfying success stories in teaching. This is an unending challenge that is never really complete. Every one of our students has faced adversity at some point in their academic careers, and we must recognize the different challenges they face in order to help them advance.

As a father of three young boys, I am already starting to see the patterns of difficulties in school for each of them. My oldest child will have to work hard for everything; reading and spelling do not come naturally to him. He is introspective, curious, and talented but takes his time to process. He will struggle in these ways, and we must provide him support. My middle son is too smart for his own good, so keeping up his motivation and drive will challenge his teachers, coaches, and parents. Providing support for a brilliant but unmotivated student is a challenge many gifted education teachers face daily. My youngest son is a victim of birth order. He didn't read as many books, viewed twice as many screens, and was dragged to every event/game/party that his older brothers attended. His skill set will be altogether different.

It's as a colleague, a peer, and, most importantly, a fellow parent that I aim to share methods to help all of us dig deeper and lean into the struggle, with the ultimate goal of making a difference.

The often-cited work of Dr. John Hattie proves there are a variety of academic and nonacademic factors that affect whether or not a student will experience success. Among them, Hattie analyzes personal things like home environment, parental involvement, demographic factors, mental health, and gender. His research extends to tactical methods used by teachers like scaffolding, backward design, challenging discussion prompts, and self-reported grades. Finally, Hattie examines the way a school environment is organized, predicting whether class size, single-sex schools, viable curriculum, or higher per-pupil spending makes a difference in the data.

Most of us could predict from experience which factors contribute most to the story of success or struggle in school. However, one surprising element continuously outshines the others: Hattie found that the most important variable in determining academic success was a "teacher's estimate of student achievement."[1] This was shown in multiple studies. Essentially, if a teacher believes a student is capable of completing challenging coursework, there is a greater chance the student will succeed. In other words, the teacher's belief in a student impacts success more than any other personal, tactical, or organizational factor in a student's life. What an amazing finding from the data!

More than anything we study, research, invest, or believe about the education system, the teacher makes the ultimate difference.

This finding comes with a heavy weight of responsibility for teachers, perhaps even a burden to some. How you view this research may determine your level of success and willingness to tackle education's most pressing issue: how to help the students who struggle the most. Since the pandemic, 1.4 million American students previously enrolled in school have not returned.[2] We can only imagine the effect that attendance has on academic performance. In

> **MORE THAN ANYTHING WE STUDY, RESEARCH, INVEST, OR BELIEVE ABOUT THE EDUCATION SYSTEM, THE TEACHER MAKES THE ULTIMATE DIFFERENCE.**

my state, Illinois, we consider students who miss more than 10 percent of school to be chronically absent. Our school has a population that has a 35 percent chronic absenteeism rate. The long-term effect of a student's absenteeism will be felt in every area of their life, from their financial future to their mental health to their interactions with the criminal justice system. Absenteeism is a complex challenge, but it's a problem we can solve. We all have students who struggle, and we will continue to have students who struggle. This book will support your desire to be part of the solution. You are capable of changing the academic and personal trajectory of your students who struggle the most, and I believe in you.

My hope is that you will find this book to be timely. So much conversation in education currently centers on what students cannot do. We too often look to the past and focus on habits that have changed; we feel as if student and parent investment in education just "isn't the same."

Some of you may remember Blockbuster's meteoric rise through the 1990s. I have fond memories of trips to Blockbuster on Friday and Saturday nights as a child. While browsing videos, we'd often see friends from the neighborhood, church, and school spending their weekend the same way. The concept was simple. Blockbuster would purchase a VHS or DVD, rent it to a customer for 48–72 hours, and then rent it to the next customer upon return. After three or four rentals, Blockbuster would cover their expenses and begin to profit off the purchase. Customers would go home happy, having spent just $2.99 per rental instead of $10.99 for a ticket at the movie theater. Both the consumer and the merchant won. Nowadays, people smile and shake their head when they think of Blockbuster. Many of us can remember the impact of this company on our daily lives but also the abrupt ending they experienced.

In 2004, a lesser-known company called Netflix offered to become Blockbuster's exclusive mail-order provider of DVDs. Blockbuster would retain the brick-and-mortar retail stores, and Netflix would cater to those who didn't want to leave home, who would instead use the internet to choose which movies they wanted to be mailed to them. Netflix, ripe off their first profitable year as a business, aimed to use its collection of over thirty-five thousand titles and one million unique sales to woo Blockbuster into a monopolizing partnership, ready to capture the lion's share of the entertainment market.

Blockbuster refused the offer, and as they say, the rest is history. At Blockbuster's peak, they had over nine thousand stores worldwide. Five years later, they dwindled to just one store. As for Netflix . . .

If you are reading this introduction, perhaps you are frustrated with our profession and its immense challenges. Maybe you were assigned this book as a part of professional development and are curious, if not skeptical, of how to support students who are struggling. Perhaps you are back for more after reading *All 4s and 5s* or *Finding Lifelines* and are eager for additional tools to tackle education's most pressing issue: how to help our most vulnerable students become successful. This book does not have all the answers, but I promise to deliver practical ideas, stories from the field, and the motivation to redouble our efforts with this group of students. I hope one day this book won't be as necessary as it is now, when struggling students need us more than ever.

I repeat: struggling students need us more than ever.

In the example above, Netflix offered a soon-to-be struggling company a lifeline. Blockbuster's model was successful for many years but was headed for an uncertain future. Like Netflix, the hope is that this book becomes an offer for you and a roadmap to change your "business model." The goal is to provide practical ideas and motivation to continue reading.

Education can be very isolating. Many of us have attended school our entire lives, and our views are shaped by our "teacher" echo chamber. This is not an insult, but merely the reality that makes us really good at what we do. In this book, I use examples from outside of education. I've often thought that businesses, sports teams, coaches, CEOs, entrepreneurs, and corporations bring a different perspective that we can apply to our craft. When leaders study other leaders, no matter what field they're in, they become better leaders themselves.

In the chapters that follow, you will read advice and quotes from over a dozen of the nation's very best teachers with track records of achieving a straightforward but critical goal of helping struggling students find success.

I feel motivated just listening to their stories and cannot wait to share them with you. They are motivating, inspiring, thought-provoking, and they will make you a better, more driven educator. Through these stories, anecdotes, and advice sessions, you will feel a connection. May this book be the start of your journey to helping all students succeed.

As I stood in our basement, ignoring the Christmas decorations I was supposed to be carrying upstairs, I scanned the letter and began to read what I wrote over twenty years ago. My eyes were quickly drawn to a list of ten rules for the team. Most were fairly straightforward, like, "no swearing," "no throwing equipment," and "no walking on the baseball field." I even addressed topics like gossip, supporting teammates, and respecting the coaches. But one rule in particular, number eight, really caught my eye.

Never use the word CAN'T, it read. *There is nothing you cannot do on a baseball field or in life. If a coach asks you to play a position you don't often play, do not tell the coach that you can't. If a teammate asks for extra help at practice, do not respond that you can't. We use the word can instead of can't.*

I put the letter down and reflected. I remembered where this phrase came from. It was a regurgitation of my mentor's mantra for my team in high school. (I believe you are already familiar with Coach Wojtun from his foreword.) We become like the company we keep, and I was no exception. So much of who I am as a teacher and a coach came directly from my own teachers and coaches.

Over two decades later, I realized that he was right. *Can't* has no place in our vernacular as educators. It makes no difference who we are working with. The situation is irrelevant. Our students' circumstances may be important, but they don't dictate the results.

Because kids can. Students who struggle, can. Walk this journey with me, and let's find out how.

Chapter 1
BUILDING CULTURE

I want to let you, the reader, in on a little secret. Originally this was the last chapter. Through the year-long editing process, we made the decision to flip it to the beginning. It is that important to the overall goals of this book. Perhaps culture seems like a fuzzy topic in education, or tangential to the larger goal of helping struggling students.

Culture is a major focus nowadays around businesses, sports teams, leadership circles, and organizations. Culture is hard to put a finger on. It's a completely invisible entity that is omnipresent in all we do. You won't find culture as a category on a teacher's evaluation, but you will see categories like engagement, dialogue with students, and evidence of student learning as evaluable qualities. All of these are byproducts of culture, which supersedes anything we do in the classroom. The gap between what we know (content) and how we teach (methods) is razor thin among teachers nationwide. Most of us know what we are teaching and how to teach it. We've studied our content and our craft for years. I really have not met too many teachers who do not have a passion and wealth of knowledge about what they teach. In addition, many teachers deliver content and skills to students in creative, research-based, and impactful ways. But in working with teachers across the country, I've learned what differentiates the very best educators from their peers.

The gap between good and great teachers is their ability to create a powerful and lasting classroom culture, one that helps students who struggle feel more comfortable and more empowered to seek the success we all hope they will have.

As much as student voice should be an integral part of our instructional and cultural design, the person in the class who drives the culture should be you. When an administrator or any casual observer visits your class, they should feel it. Culture is like the oxygen of the classroom. You cannot see it, smell it, touch it, hear it, or taste it. But without it, you cannot survive.

> **THE GAP BETWEEN GOOD AND GREAT TEACHERS IS THEIR ABILITY TO CREATE A POWERFUL AND LASTING CLASSROOM CULTURE.**

It is sort of like the adage about the old fish who swims past two younger fish. The old fish asks the younger fish, "How's the water today?" The younger fish do not respond and keep swimming. A few minutes later, the two younger fish turn to each other and say, "What is water?"

Culture is all around us, even if we do not realize it and even if it has been there forever, like the water for fish. Successful teachers know and understand that "fish swim in water," and the "water" is distinctly different from one classroom to the next.

To be clear, culture is not about comparison. Some teachers will tell me they do not have the personality for this topic, or some of this "fun" stuff doesn't fit their class. Culture makes us unique from the teacher next door, not better or worse. Sometimes when students are really excited about a lesson, they carry that energy to the next classroom, and the next teacher is left to pick up the pieces. We cannot approach this in a negative way. Students will experience something different in their next class, and that is okay. Building culture starts with an awareness it is there and an acknowledgment it is important.

Why does culture matter in helping students, especially students who struggle, ultimately become successful?

When I ask teachers about their goals for their students, or to describe the classroom culture they wish to create, the word *safe* is often mentioned. All teachers want a safe classroom; safety is pretty high on an educators' hierarchy of needs. If we explore that definition further, many teachers want to create spaces where students feel comfortable learning, sharing, thinking, and acting like themselves. Teachers want an environment where these behaviors and attitudes are encouraged. We want a classroom where students can maximize their contribution to the class and where the class can maximize its contribution to the student.

"I want my students to know that this is a safe space," says Rashida Trails, an elementary school teacher outside of Atlanta. "If my students aren't comfortable with who they are and what they share, I haven't done my job creating that atmosphere. Oftentimes, I try to model this, so students know that it is okay."

Indeed, modeling the culture we want to create often paves the way for what students will internalize. If we want our most vulnerable students to experience success, the learning environment matters. The steward of that culture is you!

EVALUATING CULTURE

It might seem paradoxical to say that classroom culture is more important than what and how we teach. After all, teacher training programs focus on methods and content. This is the process of teaching. You can have a great culture simply through processes—never make the mistake of separating culture from processes. Culture drives processes. Culture drives content and skills and how you teach both. Culture is not just about what we say. Teachers have a playbook with specific tools and methods that make a classroom experience unique. Each of us brings a unique personality and set of skills that contribute to a particular classroom atmosphere. This atmosphere—the oxygen—makes up the culture of our class.

Have you ever taken the time to evaluate what your classroom culture looks like, where it came from, or how it has changed? Moreover, do you underestimate the impact culture can have on students who don't feel like they're a part of the class—our kids who are struggling?

Some teachers gather this information from their students. You can do this at the end of the year or more frequently. I know some teachers who have their current class write a letter to their future class about what to expect. I like to gather feedback from my students on a unit-by-unit basis. Students answer questions like:

- What did you like most about the previous unit?
- What did you struggle with?
- Which class activity was the most fun?
- What lesson should I revise or change for next year?
- What did you learn that you think would surprise me?

This is a fun and informative way to gather feedback from my students. It also helps me adjust lesson plans from one year to the next. While the responses are interesting to read and helpful in many ways, some answers have led to curricular changes, lesson design tweaks, or an assessment redesign. Each of these facets of the class is important, but none are as important as cultural changes.

You can read a lot about what culture is and what it isn't. There are many books that provide both practical and theoretical roadmaps to achieving great organizational culture. To me, culture comes down to one word: habits. What habits do the teacher and the students engage in daily?

To evaluate culture, I recommend using a culture inventory that focuses on key areas of how teachers engage and interact with their students. These six key areas make up the basic habits of the classroom and summarize the culture the teacher creates:

- Student behaviors
- Expectations
- Habits of writing
- Habits of reading/note-taking
- What do we do for fun?
- What words or phrases do we use?

The power of this evaluation starts with a teacher's ability to reflect on their own culture. I use this activity in professional development sessions as a way of noticing and naming classroom practices that we intentionally engage in. For instance, if a teacher gives students a high-five as they enter the room, this is a cultural habit. It is intentional and part of the teacher's playbook. If a teacher requires all students to limit their summary writing to twenty-five words or less, this is a cultural habit. Reason or rationale aside, this is the teacher's expectation. Finally, if the teacher plays a speed-dating game with the class to help them learn different characters or vocab words, this is also a cultural habit. It is a fun way to help students remember or engage with material.

The decisions we make as teachers collectively make up the habits that determine the culture. The idea of an increased attention to culture moves beyond lesson planning, as it takes into account the regular events of the class. As an example, here are thirty cultural habits from my class, categorized into the six different areas.

Student behaviors	Expectations
- Reread your notes when you enter the room - Listen to each other when someone talks - Use every minute of class - Sit wherever makes you comfortable - Laugh when things in class are funny	- If you are on time, you are late - Ask for help before I ask you what is wrong - Check your grades for accuracy - Hold me accountable for what I say and do - Answer emails professionally
Habits of writing	**Habits of writing/note-taking**
- Use *however* and *because* in all thesis statements - Don't write things that are not true - Name-drop like it's hot. Include names, dates, and facts that the reader doesn't know - Topic sentences appear first, and relate directly to the thesis - Write legibly	- Consider the source, time period, and context - Use shorthand to eliminate unnecessary words or phrases - Highlight or underline key vocabulary - If notes take you more than thirty minutes, stop and see me the next day - Write your main ideas in 5–7 words or less
What we do for fun	**Words we use**
- Host class in the auditorium - Joke Fridays - The championship belt - Usher's confessions sessions - The "College of Champions"	- Your college professors are going to love that - That belongs on a poster - I can't teach ya nothin' if you are lookin' out the window - I am your guide on the side not the sage on the stage - Don't live life in the "woulds"

This is a sampling of 135 different habits I've listed as a part of my class culture. I spared you the rest, as they might get a little confusing without context. I always loved curating this list and revisiting it often to update my cultural habits. Culture morphs constantly, and it's fascinating to review our own development.

Creating this list can be a difficult task for teachers. Some tell me, "I don't know what to write. I just do it or say it." Perhaps they feel like they are bragging about who they are and what they create on a daily basis. If that's the case, excellent! Brag. Reflect. Shine. Emote. Evaluate.

Take this time to notice and name everything you do with purpose and passion to build culture, so you can intentionally create an atmosphere where magic happens. Good culture is devoid of ego and is focused on process and outcomes to provide a great experience for your students.

The real power in this exercise is turning it over to your students. Ask students to fill in the same six empty categories with what *they* think your class is all about. What are the expectations, behaviors, habits, and cultural hallmarks of your class according to the kids?

Ask the Author

Classroom culture seems like a really fuzzy topic. Why should I spend more time and energy on this?

We will discuss a lot of instructional strategies and research-backed methods on teaching later in this book. All of that matters. I cannot definitively tell you that classroom culture matters more. I can, however, tell you that teachers who create great culture produce the best objective and quantifiable results with students. Students learn better when they are having fun. If we can create this atmosphere in class, we will have an easier time helping struggling students catch up.

Receiving this type of feedback is critical in evaluating our own classroom culture, and it allows us to make informed decisions on what we should continue and what practices we should leave behind. When you examine student responses, you will notice parts of your culture that are clearly communicated to students; they will match the habits you noted on your own culture inventory. This should affirm your intentionality. However, students likely won't create a list that's as exhaustive as yours. Noting which habits they "missed" affords us the opportunity to evaluate whether or not those habits still belong in our culture.

Culture can be a moving target: it can be a garden that needs constant weeding or a bright northern star that lights the pathway to success. How we evaluate our classroom culture is essential to recognizing and increasing its impact. If we believe classroom culture separates the good teachers from the great teachers, starting with an awareness of what it is in our own classroom is a first step.

SUSTAINING CULTURE

One of my favorite people in the world is a priest from the parish and school I grew up attending. Fr. Bill has a real gift for speaking, telling stories, and relating them to what is most important to our faith and our lives.

I remember a particular homily he gave a few years back. He was serving a parish in 1990 outside of Plainfield, Illinois, when a violent F5 tornado ravaged his community. The tornado killed twenty-nine people and left many others without their homes, pets, and possessions. Their town—the physical history, fabric, and culture of it—was destroyed. Fr. Bill selected a reading from the Gospels and then spoke about how, in those moments of despair, God reaches out to us with a helping hand. Even though it is hard to explain how or why horrible things happen, his message was that "that hand" will always be there.

We visited him a year later, and Fr. Bill gave another homily on the same Gospel reading. This time, his interpretation and message changed. He easily could have highlighted the same story again—it was a powerful homily. But he delivered a different message using the Boy Scouts as an example. When adventuring in the forest, part of the Boy Scout honor code is to "leave it better than you found it." He related the motto to our lives, how we interact with others, and how we make the world a better place. It was a brand-new message using a brand-new story.

A really good preacher serves the message "hot out of the oven." If a preacher uses the same homily or sermon over and over, people begin to tune out. Folks don't enjoy eating leftovers day after day, or week after week.

Our students prefer the culture of the classroom space to be new and exciting. We have to think about each of the ingredients and exactly what we want the meal to taste like. The best classroom culture includes adaptations while still sustaining the energy it takes to create it in the first place.

Repeating a championship win can be harder for a team than winning a championship in the first place. Folks in my hometown of Chicago know this best. In 1985, the Bears won the Super Bowl with what some felt was the greatest team of all time. The next season, almost every player returned and the Bears lost in the first round of the playoffs.

The challenge of sustaining culture works the same. Once you create it, we must have the energy to sustain it. This is hard. I've seen principals start off their first few years with amazing energy, passion, and ideas to move the school forward. We all know the energy we have as teachers when we first start the school year. It certainly beats our energy levels in the late spring. Sustaining this energy and ultimately, this culture, is hard. The most successful school leaders and teachers who sustain culture, however, have one thing in common: the willingness to love.

I really love my students and my players. Not in the same way I love my family, but I do love them and make sure I tell them that. While this may seem corny or even uncomfortable, I've had too many times in my career and life where I've wished I could tell someone, "I love you" one more time. If you've ever lost a family member or a student, you can probably relate. There is something about the emotion you feel with those three words that is indescribable.

We cannot be afraid of love in our profession. Reminding our students how much we care, so they feel the strength of our love, is lasting and impactful. When students understand that it is okay to love back, we've got a chance at helping them in the moment and the future.

Forging an emotional connection creates buy-in with your students. Your students will trust you more and be willing to share things with you that may ultimately be a gateway for your relationship to grow. If we create a great classroom culture for our students, they'll associate the positivity of the space with the teacher in front of them and their peers. We can create this sense of safety and connection simply with the energy we bring to class every day. The students feed off the energy of the teacher and will model the investment the teacher pours into the class.

Again, sustaining this culture filled with love will test us. It is not unlike a marriage or a longtime friendship that continually evolves. "Are we going to do Netflix and pizza at home again like we always do, honey? Or, should we work out together, go on an adventure, eat food from a new cuisine, or buy tickets to a rock concert?" Or, in classroom terms, do we simply roll out the same lessons, worksheets, and game plan as the weeks and years before? The school year is long, and student attention spans are short. How do we keep up the initial passion and excitement for the first week of school that we all have and make that last throughout the year?

That is our challenge. As we hit the wall throughout the year, can we push through it and sustain an energetic culture that our students are drawn toward?

Many of us feel like we don't have the energy as we manage all the mandates of our job along with the craziness of our personal lives. I understand being overwhelmed and have felt that many times in my career. It is the sinking realization that "it never ends," and "it" just seems to get more complicated year after year.

WORKPLACE HAPPINESS

I find the research on workplace happiness and energy to be fascinating, especially with our profession and others like it. Most people think pretty highly of teachers, doctors, and nurses, but did you know that these are the three most disengaged professions in America today? According to author Marcus Buckingham, the "why" behind their work could not be clearer, and most teachers and health professionals could tell you a great story of why they entered the profession. However, for many of us, our jobs have been overwhelmed by the "what"—the bureaucratic minutiae of our daily tasks. We have to fill out reports for our PD hours, turn in lesson plans, take attendance, plan for observations, etc. Likewise, nurses and doctors are filling out charts, calling insurance companies, rescheduling patients, and documenting every development.

If we want to sustain the energy and maintain a lasting culture, we have to find happiness and satisfaction despite the evolving list of "whats." Like doctors and nurses, every day is different for a teacher. We have the privilege of working with a brand-new group of students each year. This adds life and a renewed sense of purpose to our work. We must love it.

Buckingham's research identifies two critical questions that determine whether or not we are successful in the workplace:

1. Were you excited to go to work this week?
2. Were you able to use your strengths at work?[1]

If we want success at our jobs, we have to choose joy and dig into the work that provides us the most happiness. Every day, our life is a Broadway show. There are some good scenes and some bad ones. We don't need to love what we do every day, we just have to find the best scenes and capitalize on them. Brook Cupps, author and speaker, reports that 73 percent of the American workforce must alter their work environment to find happiness. So do it. Have class outside. Read your students a different book. Spend more time with your colleagues inside and outside of school. Where there is room to do more of the things you like to do, go for it! If we can find ways to incorporate student voices in this—even better. This gives us energy, and energy sustains culture.

> **IF WE WANT SUCCESS AT OUR JOBS, WE HAVE TO CHOOSE JOY AND DIG INTO THE WORK THAT PROVIDES US THE MOST HAPPINESS.**

CONNECTING HAPPINESS TO CLASSROOM SUCCESS

So, what does this have to do with helping struggling students to succeed?

Attitudes are contagious, and your students will connect to your energy and positivity. I have seen examples of this as an observer of many classrooms. An amazing former colleague of mine, Val Berger, taught an advanced catering class at our school. A two-time cancer survivor, Val would drive sixty miles to work from a different state and arrive around five a.m. After her workout, she would prepare the kitchen for another day of cooking with the students. When she spoke to her class, she was fair, tough, and positive. She was one of the hardest-working women I have ever met, and her students began to take on some of those same characteristics.

In an era where many of our students struggle with attendance and arriving at school on time, her students were present by six a.m. They would prepare the catering requests for the day together, as they dutifully took their orders and began learning the same leadership skills she modeled when running this engaging class. The students adopted her work ethic and—more importantly—her attitude toward the work. Students knew Ms. Berger and understood exactly what it had taken for her to arrive at work that day. And they were inspired by her energy to show up and work hard. You know what's even more amazing? The teacher who succeeded her also took on many of these same characteristics, and the culture of success in her classroom has continued.

Conversely, I've observed teachers who do the bare minimum, which naturally is reflected by what the students give in return. A small portion of teachers use worksheets as a way to pacify students and keep them busy. More recently, this involves students working quietly on their computers while the teacher sits silently at their computer. This group of teachers might be more reluctant to learn students' names, engage in conversation, or design a class that reflects a partnership between the students and the teacher. We've all probably worked with a colleague or two like this.

What message does this approach send to students who may not be overly excited about school that day? Moreover, what damage does this cause to students who are already struggling?

Sustaining a culture of success involves relentless energy and a commitment we must make to our students and ourselves. This is my challenge for you: Once you create a strong classroom culture, can you sustain it? If so, you'll gain even more energy from the results and your culture will truly become recursive.

WHOLE-CLASS AND INDIVIDUAL RELATIONSHIPS

In 2017, the fine folks at Harvard University published a study they've been researching for almost eighty years. Their goal was to determine which factors contribute to three very important parts of our lives: health, happiness, and success. In other words, which factors and decisions contribute most to whether or not a person will live a long life, find joy in their days, and make enough money to live comfortably? The study tracked a cohort of male Harvard students for their entire lives, and when the study was published, nineteen of these students were still alive.

The study revealed that having close relationships had a powerful influence on health and happiness and even led people to more success in the workplace. According to the study, researchers "found a strong correlation between men's flourishing lives and their relationships with friends, family, and community. Several studies found that people's level of satisfaction with their relationships at age fifty was a better predictor of physical health than their cholesterol levels were."[2]

Relationships has become a buzzword in education, so I hope to define this broad idea and list specific ways that teachers can achieve effective connections with the entire class and each individual student. There is a playbook to achieving this type of connection, and, if done successfully, genuine and authentic relationships will help classroom culture fall into place.

The culture of each class might vary throughout the day. High school teachers usually have a favorite period and probably a more challenging group they teach. Elementary school teachers may tell you about their favorite class of all time, as they likely spent seven hours with them each day for 180 days! We all could agree that when certain students are absent, the culture of the whole group immediately changes. Similarly, one leader can rocket your class into a new academic and cultural stratosphere. So whole-class culture is fragile, even fleeting, and it may seem to be outside our control. But in fact, the teacher drives the culture with intentional strategies to create positive whole-class relationships.

One of my favorite examples of an effective whole-class relationship comes from a young teacher in the high desert of California. She teaches in Victorville, a lower-income, high-needs district. When you walk into her room, you'll notice traditional teacher decorations like posters, signs, calendars, and sayings. In the back of her room near the teacher's desk, she has a giant wall of pictures featuring her students and her. As a teacher for the past seven years, she's built an impressive collection of photos with the kids inside and outside of her classroom. Some pictures are in the halls, some are from dances or football games, and some were taken in her own classroom. It's clear that she cherishes those relationships!

But inside this simple strategy is an impactful message. Imagine a new student who walks into her class and notices those pictures on the wall. The student has an immediate and strong impression of how the teacher relates to current and former students. Perhaps that motivates the student to "make it" on that wall one day. The message is clear. This teacher values and maintains great relationships with her kids. She can sustain it year after year. With each group of students, the cycle repeats, and the picture wall grows.

Lezlie Bullard teaches English at Crandall ISD outside of Dallas, a small school district by Texas standards. She has a wall of graduation card announcements from all her former students. As soon as a student walks into the room, they see the smiling faces of Lezlie's former students in the form of these cards. The message? Students care enough about the teacher to involve her in one of their greatest accomplishments. This teacher has supported them all the way to the finish line of graduation.

These small examples demonstrate that teachers can sustain culture over time. Investing in small gestures like these showcases the strength of the relationships in their class. While these two teachers still have to work hard to create relationships with individual students, their prioritization of these relationships is front and center.

Beyond wall decorations and pictures, there are specific steps teachers can take to ensure the whole-class relationships are strong. Here are a few more ways to build relationships with your entire class:

1. Address the class using the language of "we" and "us" instead of "you" and "I." Simple changes in rhetoric send a message about the team mentality. When students know and understand you are on the journey with them, they are more apt to lean into shared goals.
2. Personalize the way you speak to your students. For example, if you are a high school teacher, "period two," "period five," etc. Some elementary teachers will call the class "friends" or "my children" or, maybe more intimately, "my babies." Whatever phrasing you use, personalize it so the class feels the strength of that connection during conversation.
3. Capitalize on memorable moments from class. It's wonderful to create inside jokes with the class, like when you recall funny and unique things that happen throughout the year. Your students will begin to respond to these humorous moments. Help them recognize how to go all the way up to "the line" but not cross it.
4. Utilize self-deprecation whenever possible. Did you misspell an easy word on the board? Spill coffee on your blouse this morning? Make a mistake in entering grades? We are human, and our class should know this. Encourage students to call you out too, in a respectful way. This type of discourse is healthy in establishing trust and helps model the fact that none of us are perfect.
5. Playfully declare each class your "favorite" class. Your class wants that label. Keep your students guessing and invested in becoming your favorite class. The habits and behaviors that we want to create through culture become easier to attain when they are motivated.

Remember, all of these strategies revolve around building culture, and culture is a key piece in helping struggling students succeed. There are students in your class who may feel ostracized, scared, inferior, or self-conscious. When we create a whole-class relationship, we have a chance to welcome that student into an accepting family—one that may unlock the secret to academic or personal success for that individual. Some students are tough nuts to crack, complex puzzles to piece together. Sometimes, it will be the commitment to the whole, not just the individual, that helps your students succeed.

PERSONALIZE RELATIONSHIPS

Forming individual relationships with students is just as important as forming a relationship with the entire class. Both are important, and neither can function without each other. I have taught classes where I really jived with individual students in the class, but I was unable to create a great rapport with the class at-large. In other cases, I've loved a majority of the class but failed to connect personally with specific students. We do not want individual students feeling isolated if they don't feel like part of the larger class culture.

One way to build strong individual relationships is by caring about what your students care about. My brother-in-law, Sam, understands this really well. Like us, he is in the business of helping others—in his case, as a dentist. Building trusting relationships is important in his profession too. People are sometimes very nervous when they step into his office.

We ran together one morning, and I observed that, each time we passed someone walking a dog on our route, Sam said, "Good morning, what is your dog's name?" To my surprise, most people answered right away and smiled as we continued on our run.

Besides marveling at the fact that he could break his breathing pattern by talking during the run, I was amazed, if not puzzled, as to why he did this. I asked Sam about it afterward and reflected on his answer. "Most dog owners are obsessed with their pets," Sam said. "That is an easy way to say good morning and make someone smile."

Sam is a better runner than me, and now I've learned he is also pretty creative in getting to the heart of what people care about. This is a very specific way of connecting with people, but educators can take a lesson from what he does, and it's really simple.

Find out what each student cares about. Care about it too.

> **FIND OUT WHAT EACH STUDENT CARES ABOUT. CARE ABOUT IT TOO.**

DEPOSITS TOWARD STRONG RELATIONSHIPS

Relationships with our students happen through the moments and memories we make with our kids. Each year, a teacher must have a "moment" with every student in their class. You will know it when you have it because your student's reaction will be one that you never forget.

Ask the Author

I've thought recently about giving up teaching. This year's class is the most challenging I have ever worked with. Can you help me come back from this?

It is easy to fall into a trap of frustration after a difficult school year.

We all *want* classes filled with driven students. All teachers want great attendance and completed homework. We work hard to create a great atmosphere and prefer that our students enjoy our class.

If we want a utopian class . . .

deserve one.

> Maybe this advice is a tad pushy, but the happiest teachers I've encountered worry less about what their kids can't do and focus more on what they can do! It all depends on where you aim the lens.
>
> Our attitude will reflect the satisfaction we get from our jobs daily. So much of our own happiness will depend solely on our outlook, our attitude, and our disposition. We control our happiness and job satisfaction. We know that deep down, we make an impact on some students that no one else has in the past. We also know that our work with struggling students can pay off years from now. This is meaningful in our profession and in our lives.
>
> I cannot fix things around the house. I cannot play an instrument. I can't fully speak or understand another language. I am not the most well-rounded man. But I know I can help others. You can too, and you do. This skill proves that you have a rewarding job.

I remember Alexis as one of my all-time favorite students. We put a lot of work into making our relationship a priority. I remember pulling her out of study hall a few times to tell her how much her writing had improved throughout the year. Hopefully these "deposits" worked to build confidence. I wrote her a Post-it note when she had a really rough day. I reminded her of my belief in her. Years later, she texted a picture of that Post-it note back to me and told me, "I keep it on my wall when I need motivation." We had a lot of moments. Some paid off at the time, and others did not.

We do not know when these deposits will pay off or make an impact. Oftentimes, students don't understand our motives. These interactions and relationships can pay off years later, which shouldn't give us any less satisfaction.

While Alexis responded positively to my efforts, other students have not—at least not right away. When I was a dean, I remember working to form a relationship with Juan during his sophomore year. Juan came from a rocky home life and lacked the motivation to attend school. I remember one day in the office, I was trying hard to help him.

"All you want is for me to be out of this school," he told me. "You know what, I am going to give you exactly what you want." Juan then got up from his chair, walked out of the office and down the hall, and bolted out the door as I was chasing after him. I felt helpless and ineffective. But that cannot preclude us from trying.

Juan didn't return for a few days, and his mom never sent an excuse email or note to the attendance office. Protocol at our school was to suspend students who cut class without permission, so when I called him back to the dean's office, he probably knew exactly what was coming. To his surprise, after speaking for several minutes about what happened, I deleted the absences from our system and had a long chat with him about building trust together.

I would not advocate for breaking school policy. Attendance is a legal document, and by changing the record I was assuming some liability, albeit explainable and well-intentioned. Hopefully there is a statute of limitations on all of this, and I promise you all's well that ends well.

Juan turned out to be just fine. He was a tough kid. We had our moment that day in the dean's office, and that relationship was solidified forever. He enrolled in my class the next year, and he was one of my best students. Today, we still keep in touch, and we laugh about "sophomore year Juan" and savor the progress he has made. Still, not every story ends like this, so it is important to have an arsenal of different strategies to use when students don't respond.

Brad Meltzer, an American novelist and TV show creator, talks about the concept of risk-taking in relationships. He believes in being openly trusting and playing the odds. No one has to earn his trust, but he is outwardly trusting to every person he meets.[3] I agree with him, in most cases. Openly trusting people get burned all the time. But a friendly and open first impression goes a long way, and it is the route I prefer with students and colleagues. I try to trust everyone until they give me a reason not to.

A few years ago, I had just finished a professional development session near Atlanta at one of my favorite schools. I pulled into a gas station to fill up my rental car before returning it. The credit card machine was broken, so I entered the store with a ten-dollar bill, hoping to top off my tank.

An ill-kept woman approached me from behind. She was probably near my age, and there was a toughness about her. She said, "Honey, ten dollars isn't going to get you anywhere. You don't want to stop again in twenty minutes and fill up. Here, take some money."

I was floored. I was humbled. I felt so small. Does she live her life walking around doing that for people? She must, if she wanted to do that for me. Maybe I'm naïve. Maybe I shouldn't seek out those moments or stop and appreciate them because that makes me vulnerable to being taken advantage of, but I would always rather start with trust. Because for the one time you get burned, there are probably a bunch of other examples when it works out.

I told the woman I was only putting in ten dollars because it was a rental car and I was almost at the airport. I think I thanked her, although my memory is fuzzy—I was so shocked by her generosity.

"Well, s**t," she said. "You are putting too much in, then. Put five bucks in and buy some candy for those beautiful boys with the rest of the money." And she reached out, touched my phone and pointed to the family picture on the screen. *Woah, lady, you probably shouldn't be touching my phone.* Again my guard went up—she's grabbing at something of mine at a gas station in the city.

The truth about trust is probably somewhere in between, and trust is probably more about balance than absolutes. We do have to be guarded in unfamiliar situations, but perhaps the more impactful strategy is to openly trust all students and colleagues we work with.

Hopefully, the story serves as a reminder that trust is powerful in building relationships; students don't have to earn your trust, you have to earn theirs.

What about when you get burned by a student? This does happen. We trust a student, and it ends up backfiring on us. Some kids will take advantage of our kindness. You will find examples of this, especially around behavior in class, requests to make up work, or pleas about their grade in class. But what about the other ninety-nine times when it works out? I will play those odds, because doing so seems to attract the type of people I want to be around. Impactful student-teacher relationships require a little extra effort, a little more trust than our students deserve, and maybe a special interest in the "projects" that turn out to be some of the most rewarding stories of our careers.

> **STUDENTS DON'T HAVE TO EARN YOUR TRUST, YOU HAVE TO EARN THEIRS.**

Building Strong Individual Relationships:

1. Individual relationships are often built on commonalities. Leverage facets of your identity, interests, or hobbies to relate to students. As educator and podcaster Vicki Davis says, "You have to relate to educate!" If you cannot find common ground with a student, take a special interest in who they are and what they are all about. This helps students feel the strength of your care.
2. Call parents to share good news and the progress a student makes. Some students are motivated by pleasing their mom and/or dad. The call will be unexpected and appreciated.
3. Take an interest in what your students do outside of class. A number of my boys' teachers have attended their T-ball and basketball games. We love that, and our boys want to perform well for them. When your students see you at extracurricular

or community events, they are thankful even if they don't express it.

4. Make promises, and never break them. When you promise to meet a student after class to provide extra support, be there. When you promise a student that they are prepared for the test, you'd better be right! If you promise a student they will pass the class if ___x___ happens, you cannot walk back that statement. Mean what you say and say what you mean. Your students will recognize your follow-through.

5. Avoid punitive measures at all costs. As soon as you refer a student to an administrator, the relationship is altered forever. Students are embarrassed when you remove them from class, and now it becomes a part of the relationship moving forward. By all means, use these tools when necessary. Just know that it will have a lasting, permanent impact on the relationship moving forward.

6. Recognize students for their accomplishments in front of others, especially their peers. Students seek the attention and affirmation of their peers more than anything. If you can be a conduit to this, it is a win for the student-teacher relationship.

7. Understand the cultural background of your student. If you aren't familiar with a custom or a culture, learn more about it, or ask. Many students identify with their culture first and foremost. If we want to relate to students, we have to start with what they care about most.

8. Err on the side of the student, always. My dad used to tell me this, and I've tried to heed this advice. Few things can go wrong in education when you advocate for the student.

9. Change and adapt at a faster rate than your students do. The school year will present many challenges, and students will show different facets of themselves to you. Be ready for this ahead of time.

10. Commit to teaching and coaching each student differently. This is not a license to have favorites or treat students inequitably. It is an invitation to find out what motivates each student in the pursuit of a better student-teacher relationship.

CHAPTER SUMMARY

Culture isn't everything; it's the *only* thing. The best teachers create a unique experience for students that drives the academic and nonacademic goals of the course. The process starts with an awareness of what you do and why you do it. Evaluating culture can start with asking students what they like about the course. I included the culture inventory as an example. Once we create the culture, we are challenged to sustain it.

Culture is malleable and adaptable. It changes as the challenges around us change and as students evolve. We must commit to sustaining the parts of the culture we believe in, leaving those that are ineffective behind. Finally, culture is closely tied to relationships. If we are intentional about individual relationships and whole-class relationships, we're better able to drive the culture with and through our students. Both types of relationships matter. Knowing students individually is a great place to start, and the vibe or buzz around your class will be enhanced by these individual moments we create with students.

If I can create these relationships, you can—I promise you. In the community I serve, my external lack of relatability contributes to my harrowing feeling of imposter syndrome. Who am I as a middle-class white male to be teaching in an 85 percent Hispanic community? If you invest in relationships, you will find a strong connection to your students and therefore to the work and the culture you hope to create. Moreover, you'll have a better chance of being the difference for those students who struggle most.

Chapter 2
MOTIVATION

Do you believe that struggling students are capable of academic and personal success? Can all students—regardless of their home life, skill set, or history of success or failure—experience some level of growth in your class? Can we accept responsibility and accountability for our students' outcomes, regardless of who the student is?

Most importantly, do our struggling students feel hopeful and capable of experiencing success, by whatever measure we use, in our class?

These questions force us to ponder our own attitudes about what we do daily. To be fair, our daily teaching patterns certainly do change. I am old enough to remember teaching in a classroom with no technology, just a mounted nineteen-inch TV in the corner of my classroom . . . but I digress. Each of us were affected differently by teaching through the pandemic. Each of us will continue to be affected by this for years, if not decades, to come. Even if you did not teach in 2020 and 2021, you may be working with students who were in some way affected. We've seen different school-wide initiatives come and go, and our approach to teaching has evolved around their presence or absence. Tactical methods like jigsaw learning, flipped classroom, and Socratic seminars have meandered in and out of our careers.

Change is inevitable. Growth is optional.

I've adjusted my beliefs about whether all students can master challenging academic work. I know they can, and this knowledge is based on evidence. Several years ago, I began teaching the Advanced Placement United States History course at West Leyden High School in suburban Chicago. We have a fine school and a wonderful community; the school is not necessarily known for Ivy League entrants or Division I athletes. Our standardized test scores are below state and national averages, and our students face challenges, including forty-hour-a-week jobs, babysitting their younger siblings, and—above all others—poverty.

It's within this context that our class test scores inspired my previous book. Those same students, from that same school I just described, achieved the highest scores in Illinois for two years in a row, and our school became the College Board's AP School District of the Year. Every single student passed the toughest exam in AP, earning our class a 4.45 average and the attention of other teachers wondering how we did it. Our students had never achieved results like this before that, and it has not been accomplished since.

My life's work since then has been to share the "how" with as many educators as I can. I've had the privilege of working with teachers, administrators, paraprofessionals, bus drivers, maintenance workers, and cafeteria staff. Each of these groups is important in ensuring the success of a school and its students. This chapter will share the advice I have on motivating others, especially students who lack motivation or are struggling the most.

WINNING EARS, MINDS, AND HEARTS

The most important thing you can do to help raise the academic level of a student is to motivate them; a motivated student can accomplish anything. The quickest way to achieve this is to figure out who you are teaching and what makes them tick.

Consider the story of Danica Newton, who teaches in perhaps the most unique set of circumstances I've encountered. Her school is located in the mountains of New Mexico and covers the largest geographic area of any district in the state. Her students travel up to ninety miles one way to arrive at school. When asked about how to motivate the unmotivated, her response certainly caught my attention. "I try not to use the phrase *unmotivated*," Danica told me. "Getting to the cause of the behaviors I observe is the most important thing to me."

Like many of us, Danica struggles to motivate her students. We've all seen this challenge ebb and flow throughout time, and more seasoned teachers can certainly point to moments in our careers when student motivation seemed to change. Instead of accepting the reality of this moving target, Danica accepts the challenge of motivating her students head-on.

In a recent conversation with me, Danica shared, "If the student is not engaged or not doing work at home, what is the function of that behavior? I have a student who is the oldest sibling of six and she has a single mom. The family doesn't have a lot of access to money, food, or time together. The student is struggling with homework completion, predictably."

In this case, discovering the root cause of motivation is not difficult. The needs of this student outside the classroom far outweigh the needs she has inside the classroom. We've all uncovered harrowing student stories and triaged them in whatever way we could. Perhaps we should begin with a focus on social-emotional learning and acknowledge that the mental health needs of our students far outweigh the goals of academic progress.

Earning their hearts before activating their minds can happen through a variety of approaches, including unearthing the root causes of behavior and modeling authenticity and vulnerability. An impactful teacher is willing to share more of who they are in the hopes that their students will do the same. Other teachers try to provide a structure for students that might be lacking one at home. Regardless of the approach, it is clear that teachers who connect with kids find more success in motivating them.

Danica creates a reciprocal culture in her class, one that requires work from the student and the teacher on the pathway to success. "The expectation is that this class will be hard," Danica explained.

> We get through this by asking questions, helping each other, and the teacher giving us hints. I put everything I have into being the best math teacher I can be for my students. My philosophy is that kids need to be working for me, and then I will run through walls for them. Even if you are staying up all night with a sick horse, "give me some effort," and I will match your energy tenfold. Your 100 percent effort may look different each day depending on your energy. For some students, not having their head on their desk might be their "100 percent" that day.

There is a toughness and realness about the best teachers I have met. Knowing and understanding that each day will present new challenges puts teachers in the best mindset. Be willing to accept students for who they are that day.

You can learn a lot about this concept from folks outside of education. Kevin Eastman, a thirty-five-year veteran coach in the NBA, wrote a book about instilling a winning culture called *Why the Best are the Best*. In it, he talks about building a culture by winning the ears, minds, and hearts of his players.[1] Translating this back to the classroom seems reasonable, as each of us has to convince students to buy what we are selling. Teachers

> **AN IMPACTFUL TEACHER IS WILLING TO SHARE MORE OF WHO THEY ARE IN THE HOPES THAT THEIR STUDENTS WILL DO THE SAME.**

are challenged with convincing students to do what we want students to do.

On the first day of my AP class, I would introduce students to a 1,200-page textbook. The core expectation of the students was that, by the end of the school year, they would read the entire thing. It was their one and only homework assignment. The students were assigned six pages of text while completing Cornell notes each night for homework. This task took about twenty-five minutes, and consistency was the key. At the beginning of the year, 1,200 pages certainly seems like a daunting task. It captured my students' attention. When I told the kids that 100 percent of my students passed the AP exam the year before, they were intrigued about how and probably why. They listened.

A class that listens empowers us as teachers.

My Aunt Kirsten taught first grade for over twenty-five years. As my own sons prepared to graduate from kindergarten, I often asked her what I could do as a parent to ensure they were ready for the transition to primary grades. "I can teach them anything," Aunt Kirsten told me. "It doesn't matter if they know their alphabet or how to count to ten. Everything can be taught. However, I won't be able to teach them anything if they can't listen."

What a relief! I thought. If I could just teach my sons how to listen at home and in school, they could learn anything. Most teachers probably feel the same as my aunt does, whether they teach kindergarten or high school.

The problem? Some kids arrive at our doorstep and don't want to listen! We have to win their ears. Part of this challenge comes with convincing students of our own credibility.

Andy Roddick, one of the world's best tennis players, was one break point away from winning a match during the Rome Masters in 2005. His opponent appeared to double fault when the line judge ruled his serve out of bounds. Roddick seemingly won the match on this call—but only for a moment. Roddick approached the referee and stated that the ball landed inbounds. The call was wrong, and Roddick corrected the referee *against* himself. The call was changed, and Roddick proceeded to lose the match. That day, Roddick lost a title but validated his character, sportsmanship, and honesty.

"I didn't think it was anything extraordinary," Roddick said of correcting the call against himself in the match. "If the umpire would have done the same thing if he came down and looked [at the landing spot on the clay], I just saved him a trip."[2]

If we want students to listen, we have to earn it.

In the opening weeks of school, after showing students the 1,200-page book they'd be reading, I taught students how to take Cornell notes and annotate everything. I repeated the phrase, "What are you thinking while you are reading?" throughout the first month of the school year because we focused on this skill daily. If the purpose of the text was to unlock all the content students would need outside of class time, then the students needed the skills to access it.

As we continued to model and compare notes, students began to understand what academic note-taking should look like. Each page of notes contained summaries and main ideas in succinct, purposeful sentences. Students practiced taking useful notes, and it became a habit.

As students began to improve, I acknowledged their progress at every step. Showing them examples of their notes from the beginning of the school year and praising their progress moved me one step closer to their hearts. Creating class time to model the notes with students earned trust and credibility.

Each time my students sat for an exam, I would sit in a student desk next to them and take the test too. I would show them which questions I answered incorrectly when it was over. Small examples like these help us make connections with students. When we prove to students that we are in the fight with them, the likelihood of them running through a wall for us increases.

The connection between a student and a teacher drives student success, but winning their hearts over won't happen without a strong commitment to winning over their ears and minds first. Then, we can leverage their investment and capitalize on the relationship.

"The number one indicator of whether or not a child will be able to overcome trauma is if they have another adult in their lives who will listen and respect them," added Danica, as we concluded our conversation. "That has to be me. That is an honor. In the position that we have, the trust that kids give us means everything."

Indeed, the opportunity to win their ears, minds, and hearts is an honor. Student motivation starts with our earning students' attention. The first few weeks of the school year are crucial in setting this tone and encouraging buy-in from the class.

DEVELOPING A WINNING STRATEGY

How often have you heard this timeless question asked by one of your students: "Why do we have to learn this?"

I've heard this question asked in many different forms. Some students prefer to focus on math concepts and insist that they will never have to use geometry or calculus again. Other high school students who have already committed to a career path will tell you, "I don't need to know this," if that material is less relevant to their profession. Finally, I laugh when students tell me that what they are learning is boring. I want to tell them, "Sometimes, what I am teaching is boring!" We all enjoy teaching some units and concepts more than others.

However, it's part of our job to convince students of the importance of our school, their attendance, their learning, and our subject matter's role in their lives. As students mature from younger ages to high school, this task becomes more difficult with exposure to work, family commitments, and the priorities of the real world. I remember sitting down with a student after school and asking her what her goals were after high school.

"Mr. Sharos," she said. "I am just trying to get through the day. My son kept me up all night last night, and he has an ear infection."

This student was a junior in high school and had already been a mom for eleven months at the time. Indeed, her priorities and her motivation differed from other students in the class. But knowing and understanding each student's situation helps us create long- and short-term goals for each kid. This student's long-term goal was the same as many of my students: to go to college and get a great job. Her short-term goal was to get through the day.

Denise Rodriguez teaches English at Brownsville ISD, just a few minutes from the Texas-Mexico border. We teach similar populations, so I can relate to the cultural context and the familial priorities of many of her students. While I search for short- and long-term motivational tactics, Denise focuses on the reality of her students' lives.

> In terms of long-term goals, many of our students don't go to college. If they can go to a two-year college or a certificate program, this is a very real step toward longer-term success. When you talk about the goals of the class, we keep a vision of college but that isn't the immediate focus. Many of my students travel to school from a different country just to get an education. Some of my students begin their day by walking to a bus stop that gets them to a bridge that is heavily guarded, just so they can hop on a bus and come to school.

Denise has an incredible perspective of short- and long-term goals for her students. Her school is located just a few blocks from the southern border. Her student population and the challenges in the community help her focus on what is really important, but also, she knows how to sell the importance of what an education can do for the trajectory of their lives.

Of course, our words might not always resonate with students, and sometimes we pick the wrong strategy, the wrong speech, or the wrong day to talk to the student about what motivates them.

As a fledgling business in the 1970s, Dunkin' Donuts struggled. Long gas lines because of the oil embargo, persistent inflation, and price controls signaled trouble for a company that sold breakfast treats. Their product was a want, not a need during this decade in America.

One Dunkin' franchise shop in Connecticut developed a really creative use for the extra dough that was removed to create the donut hole. The owner fried the dough and filled the new treats with jelly, or smothered them with cinnamon and sugar. The store owners named the product "Penny Poppers" and sold them for one cent each. Customers near this location flooded the store, and their profits rose by 20 percent. This caught the eye of Bob Rosenberg, the CEO of Dunkin' Donuts at the time. Eventually, the corporate folks made their way down to Connecticut to learn about the idea.[3]

Dunkin' Donuts' strategy had to adapt to the challenges of the times. Soon these little treats were sold for nineteen cents per bag, and they were a smashing success. The story of their naming is a fun one too. Dunkin' Donuts bought the naming rights to "Munchkins" from the creators of *The Wizard of Oz* for just one dollar. The short-term goals of the company shifted rapidly, while the long-term goals still focused on building a company that "America runs on."

Our students have to visualize a path to success, and we are precisely the leaders to help them craft their version of a business plan.

In the short term, why should students complete their homework tonight, and why should students be focused on the class's broader goals? Don't tell them—show them how reading will help them in class the next day. Many times I assigned a quiz and would let the students use their notes from the night before as an aid.

In the long term, why should students be focused on a test at the end of the unit, the grade on their upcoming paper, or the exam at the end of the year? Provide evidence from former students and experiences that prove how success in your class builds success in their lives.

Lezlie Bullard, whom you met earlier, always tries to engage more deeply with her students and the community where they reside with a connection that goes beyond teacher and student. Lezlie believes motivation comes in all shapes and sizes but that it always boils down to relationships.

"I love my students," she tearfully told me. "They know I love them. I genuinely have an emotional attachment to the kids in my room. I would fight someone coming through the door to save my children." She adds, "Why do they do the work? Our relationship is not just transactional. It is built on trust. Does this mean I let the students get away with things? No way. When I say, 'You are grounded,' you are grounded."

While we don't always know how or why students are motivated or unmotivated, we can parcel this into long- and short-term strategies for success. By understanding that motivation has a timeline and that some issues are more pressing for students, we can see our role in their lives more clearly and serve them better.

INDIVIDUALIZING MOTIVATION

If you have read *The Speed of Trust* by Stephen M. R. Covey, you may recall a story that perfectly illustrates how motivation has to be individualized. Covey tells the story of the first job given to him by his father: taking care of their lawn. Stephen's dad gave him different suggestions on how to water the lawn and showed him places to put debris. He was instructed to keep the lawn "green and clean" by whatever means necessary. His father told him that he trusted him and that he wanted the job to be truly his. Stephen felt excited to take on the responsibility, but his attitude quickly shifted as the lawn turned brown within the first week.

His father asked him, "Do you need any help?" Stephen said he was doing just fine, even though he had not touched the yard yet. The two began to take a walk around the yard, and Stephen's dad grabbed several bags and began to help him pick up garbage in the yard. Stephen started crying when he realized that he let his father down and vowed to not be helpless in his responsibility again. His father's trust meant more than anything in this situation.

If we transformed this situation back to my own home, I know one of my kids would start up the lawn mower as soon as I offered him a reward. He is motivated by earning money and then subsequently saving it all. Another of my sons would mow the lawn if I told him I would play with him the rest of the day or if he could have his choice of restaurant for the night. My third son might do it if I asked him four times.

> ### *Ask the Author*
>
> **I have several students in my class who just will not do anything. How can I help these students do some of the work and pay attention?**
>
> I am often asked this question, and I try to be consistent with my answer. Everything I have mentioned thus far on motivation applies. It's important to understand the root causes of why a student is exhibiting this behavior. Teachers should spend time trying to uncover what might be going on behind the scenes. Calling home can be a great insight into what is happening with a student.
>
> However, once all these individual attempts are made, motivating these students comes down to one thing: classroom culture. By creating a culture where everyone works, understands the goals of the class, feels like they're a part of a team or mission, and is connected with the teacher, we build an ecosystem whose values sweep the student up into the larger group. That is our hope. When students buy into the culture the teacher creates, they become your greatest ambassadors, often helping other students along the way.

A motivated student can accomplish anything. That's why individualizing motivation is one of the most important and difficult things teachers have to do. It reminds me a lot of an education initiative that came through in the early 2000s, when all teachers were focused on differentiation. We all know that we are supposed

> **A MOTIVATED STUDENT CAN ACCOMPLISH ANYTHING.**

to differentiate. We should differentiate our instruction based on groups of ability levels in our class, if not individuals in our class. We also know that differentiation is darn near impossible to do effectively. We sometimes talk about this strategy using terms from the special education world like Individualized Education Plan, or IEP. Thinking in these terms may lead us to ask helpful questions:

- What modifications can I make to help this student?
- Which resources and lifelines can I access to assist them?
- How can I connect with this student and their parents?
- Does the student need more time or different standards to pace their learning?
- Where can I give grace on assignments without sacrificing expectations?

Most folks in special education believe that students with IEPs should have as much access to the general education curriculum as possible. This concept perfectly illustrates the "rising tide lifts all ships" theory and also proves that exposure to rigorous and challenging material helps level up a student's performance. Not every student needs a formal IEP, but many could benefit from a learning pathway that suits them best. The best teachers are intentional about figuring this out and then building the road.

If you're a parent, think really hard about what your expectations are when you attend a parent-teacher conference with your own child. Admittedly, it's always an interesting, if not awkward event, knowing that you have a job in education too. While I am hanging on every word the teacher says, the one thing I look for more than anything is, "Does the teacher really know my kid?" At the end of a fifteen-minute conference, if I am convinced the teacher knows my son, I am ecstatic and feel blessed that my child is in their class. Why?

I know the teacher will be able to focus on what will motivate my child to achieve great things. How the teacher motivates my son may be different from what the teacher does to motivate the students that sit near him in class, and that is acceptable and welcomed. Some teachers spend 90 percent of their time on 10 percent of their students. That is acceptable too. When we have a strong design, a willingness to motivate all students, and great pacing through our curriculum, we can guide most students through the class fairly easily. We are professionals! It is the 10 percent of students who will really earn our extra time, where a one-size-fits-all approach won't quite work. When we individualize motivation and invest our time, we prove our commitment to knowing our students and what impacts them most.

CHAPTER SUMMARY

A motivated student can accomplish anything. If you believe this, you will become more intentional about how and why you focus on motivating each one of your students. The game plan starts by winning over their ears, minds, and hearts so that students feel like they can trust you. It continues with a winning strategy, one that has worked with students and whole classes in the past. If your students aren't motivated, change the strategy! Finally, we have all different types of learners in our classes. We don't have to give them all the same medicine. Each student deserves to be taught the same things in different ways that are most suitable to their success.

Chapter 3
ATTACKING SKILL DEFICIENCY

As we have discussed, there are a variety of reasons why students struggle. One of the great commonalities between them, however, is a set of grade-level skills students have not acquired *yet*. Each class will require students to learn content, but before they do, they'll need to acquire skills so they are able to apply the content with meaning. There is great value in teaching skills in all of our classes as we've moved into a new era of teaching and learning. Technological advances and artificial intelligence have made information much easier to acquire. The content we teach is important, but the skills students acquire in our classes will be long lasting and more transferable to their success at the next grade level and in everyday life. All teachers want students to gain more skills in problem-solving, writing, communicating, and critical thinking. If you have been waiting for a practical chapter that gives more research-based, tactical, and useful ideas, this chapter is for you.

In recent years, some of the nation's larger testing bodies have contributed to the trend of measuring student skills. They have begun to reimagine what standardized testing should look like. The SAT and ACT have undergone revisions that focus less on rote, memorized knowledge, including more opportunities for students to show off their academic skills. The College Board's AP program has been an even more pronounced example of this, cutting some depth-of-content knowledge from many of its exams in favor of skill-based assessments. In some respects, this shift has helped remove some of the cultural bias in the content of SAT/ACT and AP exams, leveling the playing field. Many of our culturally diverse students have no frame of reference for the math problem they are solving or the reading passage they must complete on a standardized exam. Most teachers, parents, and, if you asked them, students probably consider this a positive change because all students are capable of learning skills to compete on these exams.

Or are they?

Education used to focus on reading, writing, and arithmetic—the 3 Rs. Many of us still believe these foundational skills are essential to a student's success. The concept of teaching skills has moved beyond the basics, however, and includes more discipline-specific abilities we want students to acquire. For instance, humanities teachers now focus on teaching critical thinking, summarization, corroboration, and argument. Math and science teachers want students to learn reasoning, problem-solving, communication, and inquiry; these skills demand much more specificity and acute practice than the 3 Rs. Beyond this, twenty-first-century students must learn social-emotional skills that allow them to cope with and correct rough patches in their academic and nonacademic journey.

I believe teachers have reckoned with ideas like "We are all reading teachers" and embraced the philosophy behind emphasizing social-emotional learning in class. We understand that teaching is often multidisciplinary and that the content we teach is just one part of a student's education. Yet I still hear many concerns from teachers about students' lack of skills. There are many different reasons why a student may present themselves this way, including but not limited to:

- Family transience that moves a student from one school to another
- Chronic absenteeism, truancy, and inconsistent attendance

- A gap in skills created by the district or school's placement—when a student starts an academic track that he/she cannot move away from
- A lack of foundational education from preschool or kindergarten
- A misidentification of skills based on normed assessment—when a student doesn't test well but certainly has the skills to succeed in a higher-leveled class
- A gap in learning created by the pandemic or its long-term effects

Shannon Batchelor is a principal at a school outside of Charlotte, North Carolina. Perhaps it is her background in marketing, but as a leader, she refuses to let her school culture succumb to negative thinking around student skill gaps or skill acquisition.

"I am going to lose my mind if I hear another sentence that begins with 'These kids,'" she states. "We cannot feed into the perception that academic or socioeconomic challenges will hinder our progress. We have to disrupt the narrative."

Part of disrupting the narrative is a willingness to start with skills, knowing that content will be sacrificed.

What really holds us back from committing to skills?

All educators feel pressure to teach content. I know plenty of teachers who feel pressured by standardized tests, especially in states like Texas or New Jersey, where the state tests are strongly emphasized. In Texas, the STAAR test is a measuring stick. Schools and teachers prepare students all year for the weeklong assessments. In New Jersey, the academic calendar is built around the New Jersey Student Learning Assessment, taking time and focus from classroom instruction. Teachers in these states and many others must focus on the accompanying exam standards in their course. These teachers feel the weight of accountability.

If students want to access the content—any content—they must acquire the disciplinary skills first. In doing so, they won't just be more successful on standardized tests, students will have acquired skills that will benefit them in life as well.

DISCIPLINARY LITERACY

> THE FOUNDATION OF ALL LEARNING IN OUR RESPECTIVE CONTENT AREAS IS DISCIPLINARY LITERACY.

The foundation of all learning in our respective content areas is disciplinary literacy. The ability for a student to read, write, think, analyze, compare, corroborate, and synthesize in the language of your subject matter is essential. Each discipline focuses on a different set of skills. Some disciplines focus on the same skills, but problem-solving in math may look vastly different than problem-solving in an auto class. Either way, students need skills in order to access content.

I was first convinced of the importance of literacy skills during my first year teaching with a program at our school called "literacy training." I often wondered, as a social studies teacher, why I was teaching my high school students how to read. I had been trained to use multiple days of my lesson plans to teach students how to summarize, extract main ideas, write thesis statements, and corroborate primary and secondary sources. In my mind, teaching basic literacy skills came at the expense of historical events I wanted to teach the students about.

I remember when the War of 1812 was on the chopping block of our curriculum. As a US History team, we wanted to focus more on themes that drove our understanding of history, and this event didn't seem to fit any of the themes. We stopped teaching and assessing the

War of 1812 in favor of other content and skills. I felt frustrated ignoring the history in favor of becoming a reading and writing teacher.

As I would come to find out many times early in my career and still to this day, I was so wrong. The goal should always be our students' needs before our own agendas.

Mark Twain once said, "You cannot let school interfere with your education."[1] The friendly arguments over what we teach will persist in education forever. But if we look at the bigger picture, we can probably admit that many of our students won't carry their content knowledge with them to the next grade. They will carry the skills.

When my students achieved the best scores in Illinois on a standardized exam two years in a row, I found that many of them gained the most ground by having a strong base of literacy skills. It always helped to know content on standardized tests like the AP US History exam, but without the document analysis and writing skills required to compete on the final test, my students would not have been as successful.

A colleague and friend of mine, Mike Manderino, whose own publications on disciplinary literacy should become another resource of yours, convinced me of one thing:

A student is not reading unless they have a pen in their hand.

Many of our students can read. Their eyes are reviewing the words and paragraphs and pages. But without stopping or thinking through what they read, students are merely reading text, not interacting with it.

Eventually I learned that every student should be doing something while they were reading. Depending on the text, students could be note-taking, summarizing, annotating, finding main ideas, or highlighting parts of the text. For some texts, guided questions would accompany the source to funnel students toward important information. Students were required

> **A STUDENT IS NOT READING UNLESS THEY HAVE A PEN IN THEIR HAND.**

to read for understanding, but also to compare and contrast with other sources. We encouraged students to own their notes and even rewarded them by allowing the use of their notes on a quiz or test. Soon, we began to commit the first two weeks of the school year to literacy skills related to reading the text.

Nowadays, maybe the pen has turned into a digital tool, app, or website that allows students to digitally interact with the text. The point remains—all students are "doing" instead of passively reading.

Interestingly enough, I've found that not all my colleagues and peers in the profession share this perspective. One of my favorite questions to ask prospective job-seekers at our school goes something like this:

"If you have a student who is struggling to read, how do you help them, and what concrete strategies do you use to make a text more digestible?"

You could certainly expect this answer to vary depending on the grade level someone teaches. For elementary teachers, phonics, coding, and dictation could be the more common causes of reading struggles, and those skills would have to be targeted and perhaps scaffolded. With middle and high school students, many teachers see deficiencies in finding main ideas, using supporting evidence, and summarization skills. Students find themselves stuck somewhere between knowledge and understanding on Bloom's Taxonomy of Learning.

Regardless of the concerns, many candidates seemed to answer the question similarly.

"I would try to break the reading down for the student," candidates frequently answer. "I want my student to find important bold words and maybe use context clues to figure out the meaning of the sentence."

An answer like this certainly doesn't preclude the candidate from getting the job. But it also doesn't convey a robust toolbox of literacy strategies to help students break down the reading.

Struggling students also struggle with disciplinary literacy skills. In keeping with the spirit of reading with a pen in hand, let's take a look at some basic documents that can help you break down a reading. With any luck and a good shoehorn for your class curriculum, you'll have several new strategies that will help struggling students make sense of the text they are consuming. Many of them can be used with different types of text including primary sources and secondary sources, movies, graphs, charts, paintings, lectures, etc. All of these resources can be considered text.

BIG QUESTION: WAS SOUTH CAROLINA JUSTIFIED IN LEAVING THE UNION?

Text	Did Lincoln oppose slavery?	Did Lincoln seek to abolish slavery?	Was South Carolina justified in their dislike for Lincoln?
South Carolina's Declaration of Secession	Yes No Maybe	Yes No Maybe	Yes No Maybe
"A House Divided" Speech	Yes No Maybe	Yes No Maybe	Yes No Maybe
Lincoln's First Inaugural Address	Yes No Maybe	Yes No Maybe	Yes No Maybe
Lincoln Video with Eric Foner	Yes No Maybe	Yes No Maybe	Yes No Maybe

A chart like this helps students break down the main idea of different sets of text. We start with an overarching question like this one: "Was South Carolina justified in leaving the Union?" Students read multiple points of view and even watch a video as part of their text set. With each source, they look carefully for answers to the top three questions, answering yes, no, or maybe along the way. When students complete the text set, they are left with a rich outline for their argument to the larger question. It helps when teachers choose texts that compete against each other to add to the complexity of the larger question.

> **Text Coding Symbols**
> != This relates to class (I know this) + = This is new material ? = This does not make sense
>
> After reading each section, fill in the symbol below. Be sure to include your rationale.
>
> ---
>
> **The New College Economics, by Jonathon D Glater–January 2009**
> Diana Jacobs thought her family had a workable plan to pay for college for her 21-year-old twin sons; a combination of savings, income, and a modest amount of borrowing. Then her husband lost his job and the plan fell apart.
>
> "I have two kids in college and I want to say, 'Come home,' but at the same time I want to provide them with a good education," says Jacobs of Salem, Indiana.
> <Stop 1> _____(Symbol)
> Rationale:
>
> The Jacobs family did work out a solution. They asked and received more aid from the schools, and each son increased his borrowing to the maximum amount through the federal loan program. Justin, at Hanover College, and Jacob, at Franklin College, will both graduate with $20,000 of debt, but at least they will be able to finish school.
> <Stop 2> _____(Symbol)
> Rationale:

Text coding is a way to have students pause while they are reading. Oftentimes, I can read several pages with my eyes but not truly remember what I read. My mind is elsewhere. Our students' attention can drift in a similar manner. This strategy forces students to use punctuation and notes at specific stop points in the reading. The teacher can determine the stop points or can use subject headings or natural breaks in the text to delineate the sections. The teacher should determine where the stopping points are in the reading ahead of time. Students can then add the symbols and explanation to display their understanding before reading the new section. As teachers, we want students to use this tool to encourage understanding before a student rushes through the passage. The important part of this strategy is to force students to stop and think.

	GRADE Sheet	
Goals	What is the policy and what is the goal? What problem(s) is the policy supposed to address?	
Rivals	Who supports and opposes this? Knowing the rivals can help you understand who the policy might affect. Rivals provide good information; just check the facts for validity.	
Advantages	What are the benefits? What is good about the policy? What will it achieve? Is it efficient? Inexpensive? Does it make people's lives better?	
Disadvantages	What is bad about this? How does it cause harm or what unintended consequences does it create?	
Evaluate the Alternatives	One alternative is to do nothing. Most serious issues have multiple pathways to a solution. What are they and are they viable?	

A "GRADE" sheet originated as a resource from the Constitutional Rights Foundation. Its goal was to look at public policy and judge it from every angle. However, if you teach something somewhat controversial in your discipline, this form is for you. Whether it is the United States' border policy, global warming, or the benefits of electric cars, we can use the GRADE sheet to extract the most important information. Through these five stems, students can list the goals, rivals, advantages, disadvantages, and alternatives to the topic. If a student can speak to all of these categories, they will have a well-rounded understanding of the topic. Instruct students to answer all parts of the question if they can, and check for understanding that students understood the main ideas and/or the counterargument to the policy.

Multitext Summary Strategy
Text A: Summarize text A in 20 words or less.
Text B: Summarize text A+B in 25 words or less.
Text C: Summarize text A+B+C in 30 words or less.
Text D: Summarize text A+B+C+D in 35 words or less.

A multitext summary strategy adds perspective to a story that students are reading. If you present a new concept, students can create a summary with a fixed number of words, like twenty or so. As students learn and read more about a topic, they continue to summarize their entire understanding. Gradually, teachers can allow more words in the summary, but we want to emphasize using stronger words to create better summaries. A student can write, "The Native Americans and the French settlers got along well together, and their interactions were built on trade." Or a student can write, "The French settlers and Native Americans had an economically symbiotic relationship." This second statement uses fewer words, better words, and gives more specific information. We want students to do this. Students must make critical choices about what information is important enough to include in their final summary. Students are drawn to the brevity of this exercise, so highlight that.[2]

Cornell Notes	
Topic:	Name: Class: Period:
Main Ideas: (5-7 words or less)	Notes:
Summary: (25 words or less)	

The most important literacy resource in my toolbox is a time-honored classic, Cornell Notes. Above the notes, students should create a theme for the page of notes centered on a central question we are trying to address. On the right-hand side, students use headings and subheadings to guide their notes. Bold words are underlined, and important facts are noted. For each section, a student writes a short main idea on the left-hand side. I have seen some teachers have students write a question in this margin. Either works. At the bottom of each page, students write a summary of the section above. Summaries should be succinct: twenty-five words or less, and no more than two sentences. Writing tight summaries is very difficult. It is a skill that requires analysis of all the main ideas and also forces students to use higher-level vocabulary to say more with less words. While many of you already use a note-taking system, consider Cornell Notes. Whether students are watching video clips, listening to you teach, or reading the textbook, Cornell Notes are versatile enough to be used for everything.

> **KNOWLEDGE IS EASY FOR STUDENTS TO ACQUIRE. THE KEY IS, WHAT CAN THEY DO WITH IT?**

At first, students may pause when you assign a writing exercise for every section of text. Eventually, it will become a foundational habit, and students will come to expect it. It is important to build a toolbox of dozens of strategies and then use the right tool for the right job. I have a folder of templates in my cabinet and a digital version in Google Drive. Once you choose what students will read, they'll need a literacy resource to accompany it. Not only will this keep reading fresh for students, but it will target specific skills within a text set. This will help you increase student skills as well as assess progress with content retention. Knowledge is easy for students to acquire. The key is, what can they do with it?

Ask the Author

Andrew, I am not a reading teacher, and I don't have a passion for it. How can I still instruct students on the content and find enough time to teach all the skills required in my class?

Believe it or not, I have heard this question several times. We are at a crossroads in education, the intersection of content and literacy. We are all reading teachers, as text comprehension helps students access more content. Even our friends in math, science, art, music, and physical education would be wise to start with literacy skills. The commitment has to be apparent to our students, so they understand just how foundational literacy is.

Finally, texts need to be difficult enough to encourage growth. Zaretta Hammond, author of the best-selling *Culturally Responsive Teaching and the Brain*, argues that there is soft bigotry in having low expectations for students.[3] Assigning below-grade-level text will not challenge students appropriately. A website like readabilityformulas.com is a great resource for assessing the level of text students are reading. This resource aggregates several different text level sites to create a composite grade-level score for any chunk of text. Take some time to copy and paste what your students will be reading into the site's search tool to view the level of the text.

This is a powerful exercise that only takes a few moments. Some teachers may not realize that the reading level of the class text is inappropriate, or, worse, they may think that less challenging text is better for kids. I made this mistake early in my career when I advocated for a textbook that was at or below the grade level of my freshmen. My fear was that my students would struggle so much and be frustrated when asked to read it. Hopefully you sympathize with how I felt, since it's hard to watch our students struggle. My Spanish-speaking friends call this phenomenon "Ay bendito, pobrecito" or "You poor little one." If we feel bad for our students to the extent that we level-down the material, we are facing this challenge the wrong way. If you have done this at some point in your career, fear not, you are not alone. However, if we challenge our students with difficult text and provide support and scaffolding along the way, we've taken a determining step in helping grow their literacy skills.

ACADEMIC HABITS

The most foundational part of all skills students have are the habits they form. If we want students to have strong literacy skills, we should focus on their daily behaviors. Helping students form academic habits may seem like another challenge, just like becoming a reading teacher. Habits should be modeled by the teacher and learned by the students, the same way we teach literacy skills. Students must read with a pen in their hand, and we can model this with different worksheets, templates, and strategies to help them. We must model academic habits for students. In many cases, students haven't acquired these habits on their own. It is the teacher who builds repetitions for students to practice the habits they need to be successful.

Luke Staszak teaches in Chicago Public Schools and faces many of the challenges I've addressed. His school is uber-diverse by many different definitions. Luke has the opportunity to teach many English language learners in his Advanced Placement class, a reflection of the open-enrollment policies of his district. Some of his students require extra support in the class.

"There is an interesting process when you start to read their work," Luke says. "It doesn't always make sense. I've had to develop some strategies to learn how my ELL students form sentences. Oftentimes, there is a clear argument in their writing and a detailed defense. We try to help students by using documents in their own language first and then translating it back into English."

In this case, Luke must learn how an ELL student thinks and forms sentences. He must help the student form a different habit of displaying their knowledge through writing and practice patience in the process. Luke also teaches with a strengths-based approach, looking at what his students can do. He also is willing to understand how his students learn, which in turn allows him to see growth and progress in their work.

There are plenty of examples in the math world where it's clear that students need better literacy skills and academic habits. While teachers experience frustration at the lack of skills, there are varying approaches that can help students' confidence and skill sets begin to flourish. Lori Hall, who teaches math in Monroe, North Carolina, believes instilling confidence with her students starts at the most basic level.

"I have some students who come to me at a third-grade literacy level, and my job is to teach them tenth-grade math," she says. "Kids come to me all the time and tell me they can't do math. But they can do math. Basic equations, addition, and subtraction are all math operations. If we can go backward to instill confidence, we have a chance."

Lori focuses on the basics, empowering student confidence even if the accomplishments or knowledge seem elementary. Lori does not have to lower the level of her curriculum to accommodate her students' skills. She focuses on what students can do, in order to give them confidence about what they will do in the future. Both Lori and Luke experience the challenge of setting expectations for core academic habits, regardless of the skill level of their students.

All students should be singing from the same sheet of music, rowing the boat in the same direction, and receiving consistent guidance from the teacher about what good academic habits look like.

Distractions in and out of class may compound the gap with academic habits for some of your students. In class, are students seated at desks where they feel comfortable and where they can see the board and hear the teacher? Are the students around them causing distractions creating conflict? Outside of class, do students have a quiet place where they can complete work? This was a major problem when students were distance learning. Can teachers work with parents and guardians to ensure that this is a priority in the home?

The culture surrounding your expectations as a teacher comes from the daily routines you create within your classroom. The academic habits your students absorb provide the foundation of how the entire class works. While forming good academic habits may seem like a soft skill, it helps students maintain focus and discipline. We want our students' strengths to shine, and that is only possible by focusing on these ten key areas.

RECOMMENDED CLASSROOM HABITS:

1. Insist that students, when they come into the classroom, form a routine that includes reviewing notes or the lesson from the

day before. Ask them to take out all materials necessary for the day.
2. Eliminate cell phone use and headphones in class and while in school (as best you can). Use whatever tools the school provides to do this. This is a fight worth fighting.
3. Have students write down classwork and homework daily. Do not have them rely on simply checking a class website. Write it down.
4. Encourage students to ask questions by asking them yourself. Inject your own FAQs into class to get ahead of those students who won't ask.
5. Be consistent with homework assignments so students know exactly what to expect daily. Encourage them to find a quiet place free from distractions to complete work outside of class.
6. Have students recite target goals of a unit daily. It is a habit that keeps the entire class centered. These can be on the board or on the slides of a unit to remind students.
7. Do not accept late work. Bark with this one, but don't always bite when students reveal why they cannot complete something. Set the expectations high, and students will rise to that level.
8. Encourage persistence. When students face challenges, encourage them to "fail forward." Just because the student does not understand something the first time doesn't mean they cannot understand eventually.
9. Value growth over achievement. If we celebrate this as teachers, students will see the value in growth over a final grade or test score.
10. Encourage practice and repetition. No matter how mundane that feels, repetition is the foundation of all skills.

These ideas are not always easy to sell to students.

On the first day of my class, I gave students a syllabus so lengthy that it required a staple. I spelled out all of these concepts to students to help them gain a clear understanding of the rules and expectations in class. There was an audible groan as I reviewed these ideas with each class on the first day of school. I remember one student specifically raising their hand to comment, "This is the longest syllabus I've seen all day."

Over my career, I've learned to tailor the first day of school toward building trust and relationships. Still, it's important to preach these habits on the first day to ensure student ownership in the early weeks of the school year.

We are in a constant battle for the attention of our students with technology and social media. Many teachers report that student homework completion rates are at an all-time low. The social and emotional needs of our students are at the forefront of teaching in ways we haven't seen before. Teachers face the challenge of accomplishing our goals while tackling these issues daily. Oftentimes, we find ourselves in the position of being salespeople. We have to convince our students of the benefits of good academic habits. (This is a good reminder to leverage previous students and their success stories.)

The beginning of the year is also a great time to consider your grading practices and if they are fair to all students. The work of Joe Feldman in this space is trendy but important, as he challenges us to look at our grading practices to evaluate whether or not they are fair for all students. Our students should be graded on their progress toward

> **STUDENTS RECEIVE MORE EQUITABLE ASSIGNMENTS WHEN THEY HAVE A VOICE IN GRADING AND EVALUATING THE FINISHED PRODUCT.**

learning targets. For instance, many of our students receive points for completing homework. What about giving points to students only if the assignment is related toward a learning target or standard? This concept relates to standards-based grading, but it demands more. We have to assess where students are and create measurable and targeted goals. Then, we can grade that or assess the progress the student makes. We can also engage the student in this process, so they feel ownership of their progress and goals too. Students receive more equitable assignments when they have a voice in grading and evaluating the finished product.[4] Consider the homework assigned in your class and whether it aligns perfectly with the standards and overall goals of the class. Also, consider whether or not assignments should be altered based on which students they are given to.

Ask the Author

I have a tough enough time getting students to do anything outside of class. How can I motivate students to complete their work, study, practice, or contribute anything to their learning when they are at home?

This is a fair question that has certainly been an issue lately. Where does school fit into home life, and where does it fit on the list of priorities in a student's life? We have to approach this delicately, with understanding of and empathy toward each family's situation. While schools have generally closed connectivity gaps, they cannot guarantee quiet places to work, supportive home environments, exposure to healthy relationships, or parent encouragement.

That said, most students tend to rise to the level of expectations we have of them. We cannot be afraid to raise the bar. Our high expectations—coupled with modeling, motivation, and a culture of work completion—should help students invest in the

> process. Because students generally care about their grades, we can give points and praise for work completion. If we are asking students to complete something on their own time, homework should be assessed or accounted for in all cases.

STUDY SKILLS

My oldest son insists that making the leap from third to fourth grade is the biggest jump a student makes in their academic career. To his credit, last year he had a spelling test each Friday and an occasional exam from another subject monthly. This year, it seems like there is an hour of homework every night and three or four tests each week. So maybe the leap from third to fourth grade is sizable, but the biggest?

One of the challenges he faces with the increased workload is the lack of study skills he possesses. His toolbox is empty. He has not been taught how to study, yet is expected to spend time reviewing, preparing, and assessing his own progress. Watching his struggle has emphasized to me how many of our own students struggle with this lack of study skills, regardless of age or grade level.

Have we taken the time to show students how to study—or do we expect their previous teachers to have done so? Do students possess strategies they can use when reviewing material? Can they self-assess with an eye for progress and areas of growth?

My son isn't able to do any of that yet. How could he? He hasn't been taught how.

We must dedicate more time to soft skills, knowing that they enhance our students' ability to perform on assessments and retain more information. Any teacher who invests

> **ANY TEACHER WHO INVESTS TIME IN TRAINING STUDENTS HOW TO STUDY IS SPENDING THEIR TIME WISELY.**

time in training students how to study is spending their time wisely. We cannot expect students to achieve the outcomes we want if we don't focus on the process. Every student strives for a good grade, but they are not always ready to lean into the work involved with achieving the outcome. We have to give struggling students those tools.

Amateurs focus on outcomes. Professionals focus on process. Maybe that sounds crass, but I think that is the delineation between what parents and students see and what professional, trained, well-educated, caring, and dedicated teachers do. Sure, school districts may focus on outcomes because of public pressure. This is how we are judged. But in the weeds of education, teachers know and understand what progress and process look like. We can judge whether students are studying or not, just like we judge failing and successful schools. But we don't always see the work that goes into helping a struggling student. We can model this as teachers and also help parents gain more tools to engage with their students as they prepare.

> **AMATEURS FOCUS ON OUTCOMES. PROFESSIONALS FOCUS ON PROCESS.**

TIME MANAGEMENT

Study skills should start with time management. Again, this is a skill that pairs nicely with a curriculum focused on executive functioning. While our schools aren't always structured to allow time for this, we have to make time for this. This involves creating a well-structured study schedule that allocates specific time blocks for different subjects or tasks. When students at our school request to take multiple advanced classes, we have them complete a time-management form. On this form, students must visit each of their teachers and write down how many hours they will spend on each class every week. They also must factor in time for work, babysitting, athletics, activities, and family time. We try to help students understand that there often is not enough time in the day or week. By asking them to complete self-assessments like this, we can inject ourselves into the conversation about how students spend their time at home. By adhering to a consistent schedule, students can avoid procrastination and ensure that they cover all necessary material, reducing the likelihood of last-minute cramming.

Student Name_____ ID _____

Next Year Grade _____ Counselor_____

Advanced Placement (AP) Commitment Form

The goal of this form is to help students select a balanced and enriching schedule that is:

- challenging but not overwhelming
- aligns with academic/personal/career interests
- aligns with future/postsecondary plans

Students must complete this form if selecting to take **3 or more Advanced Placement classes**. This form must be completed and signed by the student <u>and</u> a parent/guardian. Students will submit this form to their counselor during their course selection meeting time.

AP Title	Homework Expectation	Summer Assignment?

Total Estimated Homework Commitment per Week _____

Total After School Commitments per Week

- Extracurricular Activities _____
- Employment/Work _____
- Family Obligations (i.e. caring for siblings, chores, etc) _____

By signing this form, the student and the parent/guardian:

- Understand the time commitment and level of challenge for each of these courses
- Agree to enroll in these courses without the ability to drop any of these Advanced Placement courses at any time during the 19-20 School Year
- Agree to participate in the AP exam in May for each course
- Agree that the student attend mandatory after school AP support if grade falls below a C

_____   _____
Student Signature   Parent/Guardian Signature

Students must complete this form if they intend to take three or more advanced classes at school. The goal is to have students reflect on their time management and the commitment it will take to balance school, work, and activities.

ACTIVE READING, SELF-ASSESSMENT, AND PRE-ASSESSMENT

Active reading is also a powerful study skill that involves engaging with the material actively as opposed to passively scanning text. I call this "fake reading" with my students, and we are all guilty of it at times. Students can use techniques such as highlighting key points, jotting down questions, and summarizing paragraphs in their own words. Teachers should look at these notes to hold students accountable. By interacting with the content in this way, students deepen their understanding and retention of information. Effective note-taking is a fundamental skill that high school students can develop to enhance their learning experience. This involves using abbreviations, symbols, and organized formats to capture key information during lectures or while reading. But note-taking alone won't help students become better readers. We really want students interacting with what they read.

For example, regular self-assessment is a proactive study skill that helps students gauge their understanding of the material. This can be achieved through the creation of flash cards, quizzes, or practice tests. My favorite website to create these tools is called flippity.net. Visit this website and click on the first link in the upper left-hand corner to create a "Jeopardy-esque" quiz game. This is a great self-assessment tool that we can teach students how to use. Students can create their own flash cards, games, and study guides using templates built through Google Sheets. I even use these with my own kids for their vocab words. The best way to motivate students to use a resource is by using it yourself. Create a few of these games on flippity.net and show the students how easy and valuable it can be.

One of my favorite study strategies is to do a pre-assessment with a blank sheet of paper. Students write down everything they know about a particular unit. They tell the story of a unit in history from start to finish. Or they can create their own math problem and solve it. Or write a thesis and defense for a topic outside the content of the area.

Start with a blank page. This really forces students to assess themselves on what they know.

My ten-year-old now has strategies to study and self-assess his progress without me or my wife looking over his shoulder. This is the way it should be, certainly as students get older and become more independent in their learning. If we are able to give them these tools, they'll be more motivated to start, commit, and succeed.

The famous motivational author Arthur Brooks said, "Work is where we build character. It is not in the consumption but in the practice of offering up our talents in the service of others that we find value in our lives and we lift up our souls."[5]

This is hard work, for the students and for us. We must passionately encourage students to discover their own skills, academic habits, and studying patterns. The juice will be worth the squeeze. The culture of your class must include specific instruction on how to study and prepare for large assessments in class.

CHAPTER SUMMARY

All teachers are focused on closing gaps. The best way we can do this is by committing to teaching skills in our classes. Our students should be reading with a pen in their hand. Active reading and note-taking will help students acquire the language of the discipline. Students also benefit from exposure to better academic habits, both inside and outside of class. Teachers can model these habits and build classroom expectations around them. By making students reread notes when they enter class or by insisting that homework is turned in on time, we are setting a foundation for the academic habits we expect. Finally, teaching students good study skills unlocks their ability to self-assess and practice outside of class. This is an endeavor worth your time, as many students don't know how to study unless we show them.

Chapter 4
BE THE DIFFERENCE

There is palpable energy in knowing we can be the difference in a student's life. In fact, some of the greatest moments in our lives derive from changing the narrative in the lives of others. My goal in this chapter is not to inflate our egos with stories of how we've influenced others—because we've all played this role with students—but in helping us to notice our own impact and thereby giving us permission to redouble our efforts. We want to build an awareness of our strengths while we invest in students and ourselves. Moreover, it will provide us the satisfaction to continue moving forward.

WHAT ABOUT YOU?

- Where do you get your energy, motivation, and drive in education?
- Where does the buzz, the high, and the fire come from in your job?
- What moves you to tears, makes you feel all the feels, or deepens your thoughts as a teacher?
- How do you keep your passion alive in the face of the challenges you face both inside and outside the classroom?

When I first became an Advanced Placement teacher, I took over a program that had experienced very little success. Our students would enroll in the advanced classes and receive a 1.0 GPA boost on their transcripts. Their résumés would look a little more college-friendly by showing they'd attempted some difficult courses. But each class offered the students a chance to pass a national exam at the end, and many of our students were not passing the exams. The goals and outcomes of the course, including personal and academic growth goals, were not met. Before I took over the program, our class average was a 1.9 on a five-point scale, and 80 percent of the students did not receive any college credit. While focusing solely on testing averages would be foolish, this part of the data would certainly suggest there was room for improvement.

You already know how this story ends—three years later, everything changed. We overhauled the culture, the scores improved, and the impact was tangible. I cannot begin to describe the pride I felt for all my former students. The product of their work was multifaceted. Experiencing success, gaining confidence, and earning some college credit while in high school was a wonderful thing.

Generally speaking, we are too caught up in results and not focused enough on the process to earn the results.

This chapter focuses on helping struggling students through the lens of our most successful students. Many successful students are motivated, whereas students who struggle may have a hard time getting started. At the beginning of the school year, I promised each one of my students they would pass the exam, thus setting the expectations and the motivation to accomplish a difficult academic feat. I promised each student I would be a partner of theirs in the journey, hoping to create a culture of "we and us" instead of "me and them."

The commitment to the work and the willingness to trust the teacher made the difference to these students. My students valued the course, the potential outcomes, and the process it took to cross the finish line. On the teacher's side, I poured everything I had into my students. My investment in their success had to be greater than or equal to the commitment they made to me and to the course. The opportunity to share in their success was the greatest honor of my career.

Please let me convince you that you are the ultimate difference. Or trust the research.

> **LET ME CONVINCE YOU THAT YOU ARE THE ULTIMATE DIFFERENCE. OR TRUST THE RESEARCH.**

I mentioned the research of Dr. John Hattie earlier, which clearly outlines the academic benefits of having a teacher who believes in their students. The study is updated every few years with strikingly similar results. Schools make choices on where and how to spend money and time. Teachers invest in different methods in class. Students present different challenges and obstacles. When determining the greatest positive effect size on student achievement, there is one consistent finding: Does the teacher believe the student is capable of achieving great things?

Simply put, if a teacher believes that a student can be successful, there is a stronger chance that the student will be successful. Conversely, our attitude and negativity can have an equally proportional impact on our students. What an amazing responsibility we share.

We can be the difference.

INSTILLING CONFIDENCE

How many of your students struggle with self-confidence?

Once teachers believe in ourselves as the difference makers, our attention turns to our students, who often wrestle with their own self-doubt. How many of your students have never been told, "You can do it" by an adult? As teachers, we have to drive the confidence and motivation for students to believe in themselves. The greatest gift we can give to our students is our belief in them.

If we zoom in further, I would guess many teachers would agree that our lowest-performing students also struggle with confidence. Recently, one of my neighbors shared with me that he was not going to take junior college classes any more. He started out with a plan to attend a four-year school, then decided to live at home and take a few classes at a nearby community college. After a year and a half, he decided he was not going to continue.

> **THE GREATEST GIFT WE CAN GIVE TO OUR STUDENTS IS OUR BELIEF IN THEM.**

He told me, "School is not really my thing. I never have liked it, and I've never really been good at it, so why would I continue to invest my life in something like that?"

Clearly, he lacked the confidence. I wonder how that was addressed by the dozens of teachers he worked with in his life?

One of the most popular leadership podcasters, Brian Knight, hosts a show focused on the intersection of personal and professional growth. In one of his episodes, he talks about the balance of results and the process of instilling confidence. He argues that confidence is born from being able to answer yes to these five questions:

1. Do I know what to do?
2. Do I know how to do it?
3. Do I feel capable of doing it?
4. Do I expect good results?
5. Will I be okay if the results are not what I expect? (That is real confidence.)[1]

Think about your work as a teacher. If you answered "no" to one of these, doubt has probably crept in.

Let's examine the confidence that it would take to run a marathon. The first question can easily be answered: you would only have to know that a marathon is roughly a twenty-six-mile run. Do you know how to do it? Sure, you could look up all sorts of training programs that could have you prepared to scale up your endurance and fitness.

Do you feel capable of doing it? Many of us would start to waver here. This is where confidence wobbles. When we hit resistance, we know we don't have true confidence and must return to the reason why.

As we think about instilling confidence with students who struggle, we have to be mindful of what their answers might be to these questions. Many of our students struggle with confidence, and our awareness of this struggle is the first step to helping them grow.

One of my favorite hobbies is coaching. My three boys all play multiple sports, and I try to coach them in everything. From team sports like basketball and baseball, to individual sports like golf, we are constantly practicing and competing. My fellow neighborhood dads laugh and shake their heads, but I just can't get enough of coaching. I am raising fifty or so boys in our community through these sports, and I am selfishly benefiting from coaching way more than my boys or my community benefits from me.

In the biggest moments of our games, it always seems like the player who is struggling must now perform. I try to pull those players aside and tell them how much I believe in them. Some of them appear shocked that I am not offering them advice on running the next offensive set or wiggling out of a bases-loaded jam. Over time, I believe they've come to expect a shared vision of success.

"There is no one I would rather have batting than you right now," I might say to a player before a potential game-altering turn at bat. As I pat my guy on his chest, I can feel his little heart beating a mile a minute. "Look at all the parents and fans, and your teammates on the bench. We all believe in you and we are all behind you."

Here is the best part of coaching this way: I truly believe what I'm saying.

My players and your students need to feel the authenticity in your voice, and your actions must support your words. Our players and students have to know what to do and how to do it, and they need to feel capable of doing it, expect to do it, and be okay if they still end up striking out.

How do we put our struggling students in positions to be successful where we can value and celebrate growth, instilling confidence along the way?

Many times, we need to convince a student of our belief in them, because it is not always abundantly apparent to the student. We have to sell them to them, and we must do so authentically.

> **STUDENTS NEED TO FEEL THE AUTHENTICITY IN YOUR VOICE, AND YOUR ACTIONS MUST SUPPORT YOUR WORDS.**

Consider this: from Bill Gates to Gandhi to Martin Luther King Jr., the greatest influencers in the world were great at being authentically persuasive.

Perhaps we can lean on the research about one of my least favorite insects to better illustrate the importance of persuasion. Jacqueline Freeman is a biodynamic farmer and natural beekeeper who tells the magical story of how bees find a new nest in her viral YouTube posts. Bees have seventy-two hours after they swarm to find and build a new nest before they die. Up to fifteen thousand bees in the hive send three hundred scout bees to survey thirty square miles for a hive site. It is quite the process. Each scout bee, just a few weeks old, comes back to the group with as much information as they can gather.

The scout bees return to the hive to perform a dance in front of the other bees. The vigor of the dance is meant to convince the other bees of how excited they are about the particular spot they found. The angle of the dance shows the exact location of the hive. If the scout bee is really excited, they send several other scout bees to check out the spot too. Within an hour, the hive votes and fifteen thousand bees journey straight toward the new spot.[2]

Will you commit to convincing your students of their belief in them? Will you dance with vigor and excitement, hoping they will follow you? Will you bring others along to create a vision of what success looks like?

The design of your lessons has to win. Your pathway has to win. Your compass has to direct students toward the new hive, or whatever the goals of your class may be.

Convincing students of our belief in them is an art. We've already established that our belief in them is the greatest gift we can give. Now, our mission is to help them believe it too. I understand how many obstacles we face in this endeavor.

Simply put, we cannot keep telling our students; we have to show them. We have to pour into their success. Here are some ways that we can show our students we believe in them:

- Seek out 1:1 conversations with them in the presence of others.
- Find students in the hall and outside of class to connect.
- Work with students after school and during off periods.
- Call home to inform their parents of their progress.
- Save student work from earlier in the year and compare it to current work to show progress.
- Celebrate progress and achievement excitedly in front of their peers.

Personally, my favorite strategy is recognizing a student in front of the whole class or team. When you recognize greatness and exceptional moments in front of a large group of peers, you'll notice the unmistakable glow on the face of that student. If you refer back to that moment weeks or months later, the student will continue to try to reach that standard. I cannot even begin to tell you how impactful this can be.

This is not lip service. These are methods all teachers can use with their most vulnerable students.

My favorite story of instilling student confidence took place when I caught a student cheating on a test. She had an index card of information nestled on top of her backpack, which was on the floor. As I walked up and down the aisles, I saw her continually looking downward and figured something was off.

When I approached her desk, I gently grabbed the notecard and asked her to chat with me after class. As the other students left the room, tears began to stream down her face and we talked about why she cheated.

"Mr. Sharos, I am barely passing the class. I am trying my hardest, and I just can't seem to stay comfortably above a D. Sorry, I know this is the wrong thing to do, but I don't think I can pass without it."

Clearly, there were some factors at play here. The pressure the student felt was problematic, and perhaps I was contributing to that as her teacher. Her focus on the grade was unexplainably against the culture we preached in class. To be honest, I felt like we had a good relationship, so I was shocked that she would do something like this.

"Sandy, what do you want me to tell you?" I asked. "Do you want me to tell you that you are going to pass the class? Okay, you are going to pass the class. You are doing everything I am asking of you, so if you are close, I am going to give you a passing grade. Would that make you feel better?"

Sandy didn't have enough confidence in herself that she could pass the course without cheating. Just passing a class should not be the goal of a course. But for students who struggle, we can define and redefine what success looks like, and it's often a goal that is nonacademic. Instilling the confidence in a student that they can accomplish something difficult is a great starting point.

I tried to channel the scene from the film *Cool Runnings*, when John Candy's character tells Derice, the lead bobsledder, "If you aren't enough without the medal, you will never be enough with it."

Sandy was doing everything right, but she didn't believe enough in herself to value the work and the process. If you cannot achieve your goals the right way, you will never be able to achieve them the wrong way. The hard way is the right way, and the right way is often the hardest way.

My job was no longer to teach Sandy. My job was to convince Sandy of my confidence in her so that she would believe in herself. Being authentic is key. It also helps to build consistency in the message. When we are persistent and intentional about what we say to students, they'll be more likely to believe what we say.

> **THE HARD WAY IS THE RIGHT WAY, AND THE RIGHT WAY IS OFTEN THE HARDEST WAY.**

MODELING LEADERSHIP

Modeling is one of the most impactful teaching strategies, one that influences the behaviors, attitudes, and motivation of our students. How we commit to the example has a direct effect on the end product.

Early in my teaching career, I learned that this strategy was the most effective one in helping my students think through social studies. Whether we were reading, note-taking, debating, or participating in any number of skills in the class, showing the students an example of what it could look like from the teacher's perspective seemed to illuminate some light bulbs. When students don't see a path, we have to either show them the path or walk the path with them.

I think the best example of modeling comes from flight attendants. Flight attendants are sometimes viewed as cloud-level waitresses or waiters, reaping the amazing benefits that come from traveling around the world. While they are trained in customer service, airplane procedures, and the logistics of flying, and their primary job is to ensure a safe flight.

Have you ever been on a plane with unexpected or uncomfortable turbulence? While it may not feel good physically, I know plenty of folks who struggle even more with the thought of what might happen to the plane.

In those more turbulent moments, if the flight attendants are calm, I feel calm. After all, they fly for a living and have experienced turbulence many times before. But imagine if the flight attendants, or the teachers, or the coaches, or the role models acted differently in tough situations.

In almost all cases, our students take their cues from us. Consider simple things like when the teacher arrives to work or if the teacher uses their phone during class time. I believe students take note of how we dress, how quickly we return their work with good feedback, and how we interact with our colleagues. They notice everything, like our own kids at home. If we are frequently absent from work but emphasize the importance of student attendance, how can our students possibly invest in that message?

"Students pick up on nonverbal cues, and without even thinking they respond in a like manner," said educational author Ben Johnson. "Body language is powerful. Show your excitement and enthusiasm by rarely sitting down, by leaning forward, and by being expressive with your hands and face."[3]

Students will naturally look up to you because of the structure of school, but many students are looking for a role model outside the home. In fact, Kearney and Levine's research in "Role Models, Mentors, and Media Influences" proves that many students will turn to media if they do not have connections with other real adults.[4] And while there are positive media influences, like *Sesame Street* and *Daniel Tiger* for younger kids, there are plenty of negative ones too. Their research further argues that educational and professional role model effects appear to be especially strong when the role models are of the same gender or race as the person being influenced.

But we don't have to share qualities with our students to be successful in modeling leadership. We do have to invest in our students' interests in order to earn their attention, trust, and love. Sometimes, we just have to focus on what kids care about.

In the 1980s, the state of Texas had a real problem with folks littering on their newly built interstate highways. No matter how expensive fines were or how many tickets the police issued, the state just couldn't seem to deter drivers from throwing their trash on the side of the road.

Then, a wildly successful ad campaign began with the now-famous phrase "Don't Mess with Texas." If you aren't from Texas, you've probably heard that phrase but may not know it originated from an anti-littering campaign. The state deployed some very strategic advertising, using Dallas Cowboys players and country artists like Willie Nelson to deliver the message. But the campaign was successful because they focused on something folks cared about.[5]

If there is anything Texans care about, it's Texas!

Student engagement works similarly. An invested teacher equals an invested student.

The late Dr. Harry Wong, who graciously wrote the foreword to one of my previous books, *Finding Lifelines*, was an expert on classroom management and instructional methods. In his immensely popular book, *First Days of School*, he advocated for warm-up activities called "bell ringers" to focus students on the objectives of the day or review material from the previous lesson. Many teachers use this strategy successfully, and research could probably prove its effectiveness.

I conversed with Dr. Wong over email about the merits of this tried and true method. In my experience, connecting with students through conversation and informal discussion at the beginning of class earned their attention and piqued their interest in an important way. Maybe I would waste the first five minutes of class with an off-topic conversation but have more attentive students for the next forty-five minutes of class. Eventually, we agreed to disagree pedagogically, and hopefully that proves that we both are invested enough to care.

"Downtime cultivates classroom culture," said Anthony Slawson, who teaches at a private Catholic school in the heart of Chicago. "There are times when we take a break and just check in with each student to see how they are doing. There was a day when we had some extra downtime and made a top ten list of Marvel movies. When your students don't have any motivation, or are struggling during certain times of the year, how do you pull them closer to engaging with the course?"

Anthony strikes me as a teacher who knows how to model having fun *and* working hard. By taking time away from class for nonacademic conversation or activities, he trusts that the students can refocus their attention and work collaboratively with him.

All we do, say, think, and design must be centered on what is relevant to our kids.

Finally, leadership can be as simple as modeling and creating goals for your students. This can be done as an entire class. For instance, our goal in my Advanced Placement class was to have the entire class pass the exam at the end of the year. Goals can also be individual. For example, my youngest son's current goal is to behave well enough to earn enough tickets at school for a solo trip with Dad for ice cream.

Many of your students probably watch videos curated and produced by Jimmy Donaldson, who is more commonly known as MrBeast on YouTube. He is immensely popular with teenagers and has the second-highest number of YouTube subscribers in the world. Oftentimes, people email him asking for help in creating videos and content online. Many kids and adults have a passion for this hobby and can also make a lucrative career by monetizing it.

> **ALL WE DO, SAY, THINK, AND DESIGN MUST BE CENTERED ON WHAT IS RELEVANT TO OUR KIDS.**

"All you do is make a hundred videos and try to improve something each time," Donaldson says. "There is no such thing as a perfect video, but if you keep improving one aspect of the video each time, your quality will get better."[6]

The reality is most people won't take that advice. They will create three or four videos and quit. If someone does take his advice and actually produces a hundred videos, that person probably doesn't need the advice of MrBeast anymore.

The point remains: create a goal and start working toward it. Students who struggle need to see and feel incremental progress, and we can shepherd this process.

One of my favorite podcasters, Ryan Hawk, began his podcast journey by cold emailing many industry leaders to be a guest on his show. One leader, Seth Godin, responded. He told him he would join the show only if Hawk produced seventy-five episodes; that is to say, when the show "makes it." Ryan Hawk scheduled a reminder on his calendar to connect with Seth Godin on the day his seventy-fifth episode aired. Several years later, Hawk reached the milestone, and Godin joined the show. Godin has since been a guest on the show multiple times, and seven years later, Ryan Hawk has produced over five hundred episodes.[7]

A key part of leadership is the willingness to create goals for our students and support them. Valuing incremental growth is paramount in building up the confidence of our students. Our goals can be short- or long-term, and they give your students a tangible way to measure progress. For students who struggle, the goals may not be academic in nature but small glimmers of hope in achieving larger academic and personal growth goals.

Consider goals such as:

- Turning homework in on time
- Putting the phone and earbuds away
- Attempting to solve a math problem without a calculator
- Attending class each day and arriving on time for a week straight

- Responding to a writing prompt without background or context before the task
- Drawing something with minimal directions
- Writing down assignments in a notebook or tablet
- Raising a hand to respond to a question in class
- Keeping their head off their desk
- Connecting with the teacher for tutoring or extra help

Many of the above goals relate to executive functioning. *Executive functioning* refers to the way a student organizes their life and the processes, habits, and logistics around it. This is the root cause of struggle for many of our students that we desperately seek to solve. Without a strong base of executive functioning skills, other skills suffer too. Imagine the profile of your most disorganized students. Do those students also struggle with social-emotional learning skills? Addressing time management and organization has proven to influence grades, behaviors, academic habits, and even mental health. We don't always include time in our lesson plans to teach these specific skills to students, but they are paramount to student success at every level.[8]

It may sound simple, but creating written goals with students has been proven to help students become more successful. Eric Potterat, a clinical and performance psychologist, published research to prove how writing goals will eventually lead to accomplished goals.

"Setting goals is paramount," he argues. "People are 30 to 40% more likely to meet a goal if they say it out loud. The percentage goes up to 62% if they write it down. If they share it with someone else, there is a 75% chance of completing it."[9]

We should note that students should not be graded solely on habits and behaviors. I remember when participation was a part of a student's grade breakdown. How do you measure that, and how can we make this fair for all students? Like the behavior of participation, attendance or student compliance are hard to fairly assess and have no business in our gradebooks. However, we should assess students on clear learning targets and use formative assessment to inform instruction.[10] Most of these learning targets can be collaboratively put together by a team of teachers, and assessment can vary for different groups of students.

I wonder how many students, parents, and teachers look at a student's grade in class as a sign of progress or a barometer of success? What if we took a step back and started to value the progress in these areas as measures of growth? What if we tailored our goals toward some of the soft skills, knowing that these goals are more tangible and attainable than earning an A in our class?

Leaders of all kinds are mindful of goals. Communicating those goals to our students but also setting the right targets gives us a chance to value growth over achievement and invest in the building blocks of what will eventually be academic success.

INDIVIDUALIZING SUPPORT FOR MARGINALIZED STUDENTS

We have all become more mindful of the inequities that exist in the educational system. Through professional development sessions, education, literature, and the media focus on inclusion, we've hopefully become more aware of the great challenges that some groups of students face in this country.

This is a difficult topic and the one I am the least qualified to speak about. The title of this chapter, however, is "Be the Difference." I believe from the research and from my lived experience that a teacher can be the most forceful influence on a student's educational and life outcomes. Thus, I think this topic merits conversation on how we can look differently at our students who struggle the most.

Each school and community can probably point to different groups that need extra support. Most statistics we read in education will separate groups along racial, socioeconomic, or gender lines to prove that some groups of students do not achieve the same as others. Clearly this disparity has existed for a long time, but only now are folks beginning to pay more attention to it.

According to the National Center for Education Statistics, Black and Hispanic students' high school graduation rates trail their white counterparts by almost 10 percent. The same website explores inequity in technology, as students whose parents obtained a college degree have a 20 percent better chance of having high-speed internet access at home. Finally, students with a disability have suffered greater drops in school enrollment and daily attendance than almost any other group in the last five years.[11] Sometimes it feels like no matter where you look, you will find a frustrating story to tell about the gaps in education.

Hopefully, it is fair, however, to ask the following two questions: Are we going to do something about it? If so, what?

I learned a little about this work from an experience with a third-party equity group in our school a few years back. The group's purpose was to ensure that enrollment in Advanced Placement classes was representative of our general student population racially and socioeconomically. If we truly cared about our marginalized groups that existed in the school, we would redouble our efforts to ensure that we encouraged and offered this opportunity to all students. The work was worthwhile and gratifying in the end, but the process of obtaining the results we wanted could be somewhat controversial.

We were told by the equity group that we had to enroll specific Black and Hispanic students to reach our equity goal. Regardless of their academic background, current grades, or personal interests, students would be auto-enrolled to meet the equity numbers we all hoped to achieve. The process did not take any information about individual students besides their ethnicity.

Something really bothered me about this process, though. We were identifying students through a racial or socioeconomic lens, without knowing if these students themselves connected with these identifiers at all. I always thought the first identifier should be "kid," and our common goal of always doing what is best for each student would prevail. We focused more on individual students instead of their identifiers and this approach was successful. For two consecutive years, the enrollment in our AP program and the enrollment at the school matched: 20 percent of our student population was low-income Hispanic males, and 21 percent of our enrollment in our AP program was low-income Hispanic males. Win!

We did not accomplish this by focusing on demographics. Instead, we focused on our individual students, getting to know them, reaching out to parents, and bringing a team of people together to make enrollment recommendations. That helped us reach statistical equity.

So what can we learn from this outcome?

We have to try to individualize support for students as much as we can, regardless of which group they may belong to. Personalizing education helps students become more independent learners, better prepares them for the future, and allows educators to address learning gaps more effectively.[12] Furthermore, the connection between academic success and student interest is obvious. By strengthening student agency with a more personalized pathway, we give students permission to find their passion. By focusing on individualized learning plans, educators can create an inclusive and supportive environment that acknowledges and addresses the unique needs of each student, fostering a more equitable educational experience.

One example of how this worked was our problem-solving process. Students were referred by a teacher or by survey data to our student services team. We would use a problem-solving form to gather data about the student to begin to individualize support. Over time, we built an exhaustive list of interventions that we could specifically prescribe to the student. These included:

- Math and writing center pass
- Counselor group
- Check in-check out
- Parent meeting
- Peer mediation
- Preferential seating

- Refer to nurse
- "Anytime" pass to student services
- Connect to extracurriculars
- Adult mentor program
- Learning center access
- Teacher office hours
- Work prioritization document
- Tapestry program
- Schedule change
- 504/Assessment

These interventions represent just a fraction of what we could offer struggling students. The most important part of the process was individualizing support for students and understanding how each situation was different. We can only do that by engaging with the student and having them engage more with their own struggles.

The magic with students happens first through 1:1 connections. Whether students are deciding how or if to complete their homework, or which class to enroll in, the individual conversation will go a long way in influencing the final outcome. When we worked to improve our equity in the AP program, we reached out to every student with a GPA over 2.0 to gauge their interest in AP courses. We wrote them cards and placed them in their lockers. Our team printed *We Want You for AP* posters all over the school. We tried to support, recruit, and individualize our efforts to make our program more equitable. That is how we built a more inclusive, equitable program that encouraged all students to take ownership in their course placement.

Casey Soto's approach to individualizing support is really creative. She teaches at La Cueva High School in Albuquerque. She finds that students seek individual support after school but tries to flip this practice by focusing on in-class support.

"The goal is to get our students to ask for help *during* class," she says. "The other students need to see that it is okay to struggle and that I am there to help. The real value is getting other students to see this. Moreover, there is another layer of kids who will never speak up, before, during, or after class. I have to show all the students that speaking up and asking for help gets you the individual support you need."

Casey's approach is steeped in differentiation. She will give different prompts, assignments, and/or direction adaptations to the students who need it most.

Despite this, some of you reading will argue that individual attention isn't enough. I understand that. If we want justice in our education system, we have to specifically champion new opportunities for marginalized groups of students to create a more fair and equitable school. If that is the case, I would argue that we take a hard look at what we are doing to reach out to our largest and most obvious subgroup that is struggling.

Before I went into the teaching profession, my dad gave me all sorts of advice on what life was going to be like as an educator. He had thirty-eight years of experience. So if he spoke, I listened—although he might argue otherwise. One thing that struck me was his insistence that girls made better students than boys. He had no evidence, probably no data, and probably spoke at a time when generalizing was more socially acceptable.

I've already shared some of my personal story, so knowing I have three sons and I coach the rest of the boys in our community may soften the argument I'll make about the gender achievement gap. There's also a large body of compelling research I hope will persuade you.

Richard Reeves is a senior fellow at the Brookings Institution in Washington, DC, and is the author of multiple books on this very topic. Most recently he wrote a book called *Of Boys and Men: Why the Modern Male Is Struggling, Why It Matters, and What to Do about It*. His research focuses on a topic that runs as a counternarrative toward popular thought. As a society, we are quick to point out the lack of female representation in politics, leadership, and many professions.

There is plenty of research to support this, and anyone who talks about this inequity probably does so justifiably.

On the flip side, have we spent enough time thinking about what my father claimed years ago?

Reeves points out several distressing facts about our male students and the trends facing the gender achievement gap in education today. Unfortunately for boys, they are behind in almost every category:

- College enrollment today is now 60 percent female and 40 percent male. This contrasts with the 1972 statistic that 53 percent of college enrollees were males.
- In 1972, women were 13 percent less likely to graduate college in four years than men. Today, men are 15 percent less likely to graduate college in four years than women.
- In American high schools, the top 10 percent of the class is two-thirds girls, and the bottom 10 percent is made up of two-thirds boys. In addition, females lead males in important categories like attendance and homework completion and are less often referred for discipline.
- There has been a steady decline in the last twenty years of male teachers in K–12 education.
- American men today earn less than American men did in 1979, factoring in inflation and earnings distribution.
- The average American male who graduates high school in the same area where his father graduated high school will not be expected to do as well, economically speaking, as his father did.[13]

"These are the boys that loving mothers and families give to us, entrusting that we can help raise them to be chivalrous in a house fire but presentable at a dinner party," says Reeves.

What a challenge for us all! While this group's performance is certainly alarming, it is not always the common narrative we hear about in education. Should it be?

How can we individualize our support for boys?

For starters, we have to connect. What do our boys want? How do they express it? How can we extract this information in order to solve the problem? Boys aren't always willing or able to answer direct questions about their wants and needs. Here are some actionable steps you can take with boys who are struggling, but who may not let you know why:

- Boys love attention. Openly give them attention in front of others for positive things they accomplish. This helps build a connection and a relational trust with your male students.
- Boys love attention (again). Do not give them negative attention in front of their peers and friends. Try to have critical conversations with them on the side. We never want to embarrass them in front of their peers.
- Boys love their moms. Try to make contact with a female figure in your male student's life. It may offer insight into what he needs most.
- Boys love humor. Their sophomoric and oft-lagging maturity opens the door to humor. Swing that door wide open in hopes of keeping your boys feeling comfortable.
- Boys accept challenges. Teenage boys filled with testosterone are more motivated and seek dominance when challenged.[14]

One of my favorite schools in the world is Radford High School on the island of Oahu in Hawaii. The school is located just a few miles from Pearl Harbor, and a majority of the students are from military families. The school reports that just 20 percent of their students will spend all four years at the school, with the other 80 percent moving in and out of the community depending on their families' military orders.

The teachers and administration at this school have to think about everything differently, knowing that their students may only be with them for a brief time. What role does the school play in the development of these students, and how can the school make a lasting contribution to their education? Your school, too, may be challenged with a transient student population.

We have to ask questions. We must value data. We have to alter our game plan based on who needs the most support.

Whether we are talking about students who are Black, Hispanic, poor, male, or transgender, we all can be positive forces in our students' lives. In my narrow view, we cannot see students through these identities or statistics. We cannot do things in the name of equity. We cannot reach out to one group and ignore another. This is not a license to be color-blind. However, this approach encourages teachers to address cultural differences in a more nuanced and individualized way, recognizing that individuals within a racial or socioeconomic group can have diverse experiences and needs.[15]

> WE HAVE TO ASK QUESTIONS. WE MUST VALUE DATA. WE HAVE TO ALTER OUR GAME PLAN BASED ON WHO NEEDS THE MOST SUPPORT.

They are all our kids. The more we focus on an individual path for our students, the better chance these students have to become successful. We can only find an individual path by knowing and understanding who our students are.

Consider the story of the salesman who pitches to a room of twelve very powerful women in CEO positions. He enters the room extremely nervous, wearing a shirt that doesn't match his pants and a tie that needs some adjustments. He begins by clearing his throat and taking a drink of water, spilling a few drops down his chin onto his shirt. The salesman reads his slides word for word and only looks up from his computer a few times, making very little eye contact with his audience.

How many of you might think this salesman would be successful given his audience and his performance?

Amazingly, the salesman made the sale! Despite his shabby appearance and poor speaking skills, his entire inventory sold out.

Context is certainly important, as is knowing the audience and the entire story. What if I were to tell you that the "salesman" was a seven-year-old boy selling chocolate chip cookies that he personally baked…to twelve mothers? Perhaps the results would be more understandable, if not entirely likely.

Knowing our audience, connecting with their wants and needs, and tailoring our instruction to our "customers" are all strategies that can help struggling students become more successful.

How do you present information to students? Are they engaged in learning—excited about today's lesson? How do you convince students to buy what you are selling? What are the first five minutes of class like, and what impressions do students have after the first week of class?

If we focus on how a teacher can relate to their students or, in this case, a salesman to his audience, it may add context to who the students are and where they come from. Knowledge of the whole story, the context, and the history not only explains certain behaviors and habits our students display but helps us find solutions. We aren't looking to make excuses for our students. We are looking for the right recipe for success, knowing that we can make the ultimate difference.

Does that mean we spend more time after school with certain students? Does it mean we call some parents more often? Can a teacher give a student a chance to make up an assignment to show learning and growth? Do we go the extra mile to figure out what is happening at home? Most importantly, do we value the soul and spirit of each student and endlessly pursue the path that will help them the most?

The answer is yes.

If we want to help groups of students who struggle the most, we must individualize support.

CHAPTER SUMMARY

As educators, we can be the reason why students succeed, and Hattie's research will prove that the teacher can also be the reason a student struggles. If we believe students who struggle can achieve academic and personal growth, we must help students believe it themselves. The greatest gift we can give our students is our belief in them. This will only carry weight, however, if we model good habits and attitudes around our students. Setting goals with students and valuing progress over achievement defines the journey. Finally, challenging all students individually, honoring who they are and where they come from, and building an awareness of their cultural backgrounds helps us create greater equity in our schools.

Chapter 5
ASSESSMENT, HOMEWORK, AND THE USE OF DATA

"How do you know that they know?"

I was stunned when my evaluator asked me this question during our meeting after my first evaluation as a new teacher. It is important to constantly assess student progress. Years later, when I evaluated teachers as an assistant principal, I asked the same exact thing. Phrasing it this way was important to me, because assessment is a two-way street. Many teachers and the increasing majority of administrators use assessment to determine if their students are progressing. The best teachers use assessment to determine if they themselves are progressing in how they present material.

The merits and fairness of standardized testing are certainly up for debate and have come into greater focus as colleges eliminate the requirement to submit them in the application process. However, we would probably feel inclined to share our students' performance with the world if we felt pride in it. Feeling pride in student achievement in and of itself is a nod to the importance of data in our profession.

I get it. Assessment is not the most exciting topic, and most of us are tired of hearing about it. Many of us feel that it detracts from the valuable time we have to teach our students. We all feel shackled by state mandates and the additional pressure from administrative or district initiatives. But when we close the classroom door, it is our show, and it is our job help students make progress no matter what the test scores might suggest.

Data is the way that students whisper in our ears. While we can often point to different reasons why students are successful or not, the hard data guides our course of action. Many schools feel that they are data rich but action poor. We have the access to the data that helps us ask many questions, but oftentimes, we fall short in following through on our solutions.

This chapter is an exploration of how cumulative assessment helps students remember and retain important skills and content. We will discuss the role that assessment plays in our classrooms and how we can use this data to drive our plan of action with individual students and the class as a whole. We too often find ourselves caught between valuing growth or achievement. While both are important, I'll make a case that growth matters most.

> **DATA IS THE WAY THAT STUDENTS WHISPER IN OUR EARS.**

CUMULATIVE ASSESSMENT

One of the hallmark instructional practices in my first book, *All 4s and 5s: Teaching and Leading Advanced Placement Programs*, focuses on assessing students cumulatively. As an Advanced Placement teacher, retention was paramount in a class that tests students on information acquired over the entire year. The final exam does not discriminate between the course content learned in August versus content learned in May. Yet students always seemed to perform better on recent content rather than concepts learned in the first semester. The advantages of retention cannot be overstated, and review strategies help students hold their learning for longer.

Sam Dowrey, who teaches science in suburban Denver, reminded me that some classes, like his, are built for cumulative review. "With many math and science classes, if you do not learn concepts or skills the first time, you won't be able to move to the next unit," he said. "Everything we do is cumulative, and this goes a lot farther back than high school or middle school. If you don't know addition, you cannot learn subtraction."

I would think that foreign language teachers would agree, as would art teachers, industrial tech teachers, and those who teach anything with writing. Elementary school teachers are always hopeful that skills are accumulating. We hope to build on skills students have already learned in order to forge new learning.

We know that students who struggle might have gaps in their education due to poor attendance. When students are not in school, it creates disjointed learning that we desperately try to address when they return. Perhaps we should focus more on retention of skills and content in order to keep the foundation of learning strong.

The advantages of dedicating time to memory and retention are well-documented. Drs. Robert and Elizabeth Ligon Bjork are both clinical psychologists at the University of California, Los Angeles. Their research concludes that learning has a direct connection to memory and that the optimal conditions for learning are achieved through spacing of information and a focus on memory retention.[1] Furthermore, both researchers explore the idea of a "learning plateau," where students who are not consistently exposed to and challenged by previously learned material lose the knowledge.

Memory and retention are important staples of preventing learning plateaus. What does this look like in practice for teachers?

I toyed with this idea as a classroom teacher myself. Whether I was teaching an Advanced Placement class or the lowest level of US History that our school offered, I tried to remain committed to making old material new for my students.

Our unit exams typically consisted of fifty questions that would mirror how the College Board assessed my students at year's end. In a lower-level class, I would give my US History students forty questions that mimicked the final exam at the end of the course. In short, each unit's assessment would be a mini-version of the final assessment, using the same style of questions and timing required to complete it. However, in both of these classes, the first half of the exam would include questions from the current unit, and the second half of the exam included questions from previous units throughout the year.

For example, the unit eight exam featured twenty-five questions from unit eight and twenty-five questions from units one through seven. The review questions might even be written the exact same way they had been written on previous exams. Sometimes, I would change the order of the answers. Other times, I would ask brand-new questions. The point was that students would constantly encounter questions, themes, and concepts from previous units. By the end of the school year, most students "aced" that portion of the exam, having been exposed to the questions multiple times throughout the year. Testing cumulatively also forces students to correct mistakes before the next unit to avoid missing the same question many more times. When we build knowledge and retain it, we want to avoid doing so on a faulty platform.

A group of teachers at South Gwinnett High School outside Atlanta committed to this type of cumulative testing. Students in their classes could expect to see review questions on all of their assessments. Once it was the norm, students became accustomed to the practice and the culture around the school began to shift. Students began to expect a consistent assessment practice from their teachers. The class and the teacher might change, but the culture around assessment stayed the same. This is the type of practice that school leaders love to see. When instructional practices and assessment are consistent across classes, kids win. Learning never stops, and retention provides a solid base for additional concepts.

> **WHEN INSTRUCTIONAL PRACTICES AND ASSESSMENT ARE CONSISTENT ACROSS CLASSES, KIDS WIN.**

I also found ancillary benefits to assessing my students this way. For starters, many students experienced a reduction in test anxiety. Students could be certain of what half of the test included. In addition, this style of assessment helps to eliminate the "cramming" mentality. Regular review and exposure to the same material builds familiarity and eliminates the need to learn concepts at the last minute. Finally, cumulative assessment gave me a more holistic evaluation of student progress. Those of us seeking a mastery learning or standards-based learning model will gain a more comprehensive overview of a student's progress over time. Valuing growth over achievement is not only a growing trend in our field but one that honors the place where students are when they enter our class, rewarding all of us for how far we can take them.

And if the students perform poorly on the cumulative exam?

"I do believe in retakes, but I don't believe in the way often administrators preach," said John Elfner, who teaches in the southern suburbs of Chicago. "Many times I feel like we retest students just to get them to pass, so it looks good. This is not a philosophy, but more of a way to get A's and B's. I believe in retakes in the same way as a coach believes in making you shoot more to become a better shooter. I want my students to practice on their own and achieve a certain score before I even let them retake it."

The final grade should not matter as much as what the final proof of learning looks like. Students in Elfner's class must log into the practice portal or a third-party quiz website and show proof of their score increases before they can retake the test. In the same way we value the process of retention, he values the process of arriving at course standards.

> ### Ask the Author
>
> **There is a de-emphasis on standardized tests and assessments in the educational community. We already test kids too much. Why should standardized testing matter, and how do they help students who struggle?**
>
> It is certainly understandable to feel this way. My godson, Massi, lives in London and is in fifth grade. He is assigned three times the amount of homework and takes three times the exams that my fifth-grade son does here in the United States. I cannot believe how much schools assess students abroad, so perspective does matter.
>
> For students, standardized testing and assessments are an opportunity to grow confidence and resilience, which supports intrinsic motivation and a self-awareness that will benefit our students outside the classroom. I also think this relates to the idea of goal setting with students, where they can self-assess their performance but also create goals with the teacher.
>
> For teachers, tests and assessments measure the effectiveness of our instruction. Reflecting on the data and analyzing student performance gives us the pedagogical adaptability that the best teachers possess. We can also use these results to create a 1:1 learning pathway for each of our students.

Demonstrating retention can take many shapes and forms, depending on which subject and grade level we teach. Oftentimes, English teachers ask me how they can accomplish this when the main objective of their class is to help students grow by writing. But writing is a process, built first with brainstorming, drafting, outlining, writing thesis statements, supporting evidence, and building connections between ideas. Certainly students who can write an entire rhetorical analysis by year's end could benefit from returning to the building blocks of outlining and sharpening a thesis statement. Forcing students to return to the roots of what they learn reinforces important concepts and encourages a culture of continuous engagement with your class material.

Cumulative assessment not only helps your students retain information but also increases their confidence through witnessing their own learning. The "spacing effect" refers to the phenomenon where learning is enhanced when assessment is spaced out over time rather than massed together. Cumulative testing inherently incorporates spacing by revisiting material from previous units or topics, which can lead to better long-term retention compared to cramming or massed practice.[2] When students revisit previous topics, we give them an opportunity to relearn, learn, or practice previous material. You will instantly notice the attitude students have toward "previous" topics. Nothing is a previous topic—they are responsible for it moving forward.

Ask the Author

We have common assessments, or my assessments have to align with the state standards. How can I still cumulatively assess?

We can include questions from previous units as long as they are in the same format as the common assessment or state exam. Students do need the exposure, timing, and stamina practice for the final exam. If your course team uses common assessments, I would consider using the research to advocate for continuous engagement in the material of the course. If that does not work with the team, you could use small assessments or quizzes on past material. This will serve as an assessment of how much information and skills your students have retained, and how much reteaching may be necessary.

Furthermore, cumulative testing often involves weaving (or "interleaving") different topics or units within the same assessment. Interleaved practice, where classroom practice sessions alternate between different topics, has been shown to enhance learning and transfer of knowledge.[3] I used to love including questions about the causes of the civil war, Reconstruction, or Jim Crow laws when students learned about the civil rights movement. Though the topics were a hundred years apart, the roots of the civil rights movement were addressed in previous units. Assessments would include questions from those previous units, knowing they would connect perfectly with what the current unit covered.

The goals of cumulative assessment are varied. If we promote long-term memory, enhance our students' ability to retrieve skills and information, or help them integrate their past knowledge with the previous unit, it is a win.

HOMEWORK

The role of homework in education has been a topic of national discussion for at least twenty-five years now. The flipped classroom phenomenon helped us all reimagine how we could best use our class time. Typically, teachers have great autonomy over what they assign students to complete outside of class. The trend against homework was probably exacerbated by a worldwide pandemic that saw teachers and students value class time more than ever.

As my sons grow older, my wife has taken on a second job of helping them with their homework. She does not receive a 1040 form at the end of the year, but she does invest a lot of her time alongside the boys while they work. This, of course, happens during the tight hour-long window between school, dinner, and a practice or game. It happens nightly, a routine that makes us all long for summer.

As the classroom material becomes more challenging, parents are left to follow assignments and grades online, hoping their additional prodding will motivate their child to complete work. I can understand the frustration that parents face over the lost family time to all of this additional work. Some of us have experienced this as parents—even taking homework on vacation or over long breaks.

The research on the effectiveness of homework is conflicting and dated. Harris Cooper's famous study from 1987 to 2003 proved that homework was more effective when assigned in high school and middle school than in elementary school.[4] Other studies highlight the negative relationship between the amount of homework assigned and students' well-being. Excessive homework loads may contribute to stress and anxiety among students, particularly students in advanced classes who take their grades and learning very seriously. Again, some teachers are successful in assigning homework and having students complete it. Other teachers don't assign homework, and students still achieve the goals of their course. There is no judgment on where you stand.

Of course, at the center of this discussion are the students themselves. Many of our students are committed to other activities after school, including sports, the arts, religious education, and other hobbies they may enjoy. Older students work to support themselves and their families. Many of my high school students babysit their younger siblings. In addition to their forty-hour "job" of going to school, students are being asked to do even more with homework.

We have to be understanding of the role that homework plays in the lives of our students. At the same time, we cannot use this as an excuse for students not to practice, read, write, or engage with the goals of your class. There is no excuse for lowering standards.

> ### *Ask the Author*
>
> **I do not give or believe in homework. Am I short-changing my students?**
>
> In a word, no. In more words, I would want to look deeper into your goals and desired outcomes and whether or not students are meeting those. Some of the most successful teachers I have worked with do not assign homework. Especially today, we have to focus on accomplishing as much as we possibly can during class time. This also offers us the opportunity to give students the best feedback. We want students to demonstrate their knowledge in front of the teacher. In fact, more teachers are turning to this idea because of AI and the ease with which students can cheat on their work. The more students accomplish in class, the more oversight the teacher has in the process and the more capable they are of giving students instant feedback. There is value in many different approaches to homework.

In the 1980s, American engineer and designer David Kelley and his fledgling company, called IDEO, provided some of the designs for successful companies like Apple. Part of their pitch was a concept called "design thinking," a process by which creators put their end users at the center of their design. As Apple began to design phones, they asked consumers what features they wanted.

The premise of design thinking, which was later adopted by Stanford University as a problem-solving method, is to empathize with the end user of a product. In our case, the end users are our students. Have we stopped to take inventory of what our students want and need? Do we empathize with their busy lives and the role that homework may play? Can we balance the goals of the course and the mental health of our kids?

Sometimes all we have to do is ask.

Apple's future CEO knew this too. Always interested and inquisitive, Steve Jobs was looking for some spare electronics parts to build a frequency counter in his home. He found a phone book and looked up the information for Bill Hewlett, the cofounder of the tech giant Hewlett-Packard. To his surprise, Hewlett answered the phone and chatted with Jobs for twenty minutes. A few days later, the two struck up a conversation at Hewlett's home. Jobs walked away with the parts he needed, and Hewlett walked away impressed by the gumption of this young man. A week later, Bill Hewlett offered Steve Jobs a summer internship at HP. Steve Jobs was only twelve years old, and the rest was history.[5]

As Jobs reflected on his humble beginnings, he noted, "Most people don't get these experiences because they never ask. The secret is to make the call. Most people never ask, and sometimes that's what separates the people that do things from the people that just dream about them."[6]

If you ask your students about homework, many of them will probably request that it not be assigned. But a more rational conversation may lead you to a homework policy that I've used and still advocate for today.

What is the one thing you want students to complete with regularity and consistency throughout the year? Pick just one thing. It should be skill-based and should also directly align with the most important goals of your course. In my class, students were assigned the textbook to read and take Cornell notes. There were no group projects, no videos to watch or primary sources to read. Students did not have to write at home, research online, or finish questions 3–5 because we didn't accomplish that in class.

So that covers homework, but what about other hallmarks of your instructional practice? When it comes to designing our instructional practices for struggling students, we have to be mindful of what they want and how we empathize with their challenges. Knowing that the policies in my class had to work for everyone, I asked students about the following areas of my class design. All of your policies and ideas should be amended to fit the needs of an individual student who is struggling. Once I asked students more about each topic, I learned a lot more about what they needed most. Now, the instructional practices looked like this:

Topic	Student response	My instructional adjustments
Homework	"We don't want homework."	Students receive one simplified and purposeful assignment but no others.
Informal assessment	"We won't do homework or in-class assignments unless it is for a grade."	We assign quizzes and checks for understanding that help student grades (what students want). More importantly, they advance student learning (what I want).
Mastery learning/extra credit	"We want the best grade possible, and if we mess up, we want a second chance."	I allow students to rewrite, retake, or retest everything for half the points back.
Assessment	"We want some sections of the test to be easier to give us confidence."	Half the questions on the exam will be review questions students have seen before.
Feedback	"We want personal feedback."	Students will conference with me about their work. I can tell them more in five minutes than my red pen can write in twenty.
Review	"Can you go over this again?"	Each assessment will have a half-class period of review, and we will review for state/national exams for a week at the year's end.

Homework is perhaps the most pronounced of these concepts on the chart. Homework should be simplified and valuable to students. By reducing what we ask students to complete to one task, students see the importance and relevance of the homework. If a teacher's lesson plan before and after homework relates to the homework itself, students will see the connection. Teachers can also quiz students formally on their one assignment, as many students will care about their grade more than just doing homework. It will also help teachers assess how many students are completing the work and whether or not some reteaching might be in order.

There are other ancillary benefits to students completing the homework you assign, if you do assign homework. We've discussed the soft skills students need to stay organized and on-task, as well as the importance of goal setting and learning study skills. Students who struggle need all the help they can get to learn in these areas. Completing homework teaches students valuable skills such as responsibility, time management, and self-discipline. By completing assignments independently and meeting deadlines, students learn to take ownership of their learning and develop important life skills that are essential for success beyond school.[7]

If these thoughts seem old-school, maybe they are. Robert Burdick, who teaches chemistry outside Tampa, Florida, describes himself as old-school. He teaches in a high-needs school of 2,500 students. With Florida's teacher salaries among the lowest in the country and the poverty rate among the highest, Burdick's students defy the odds and pass the state exam at nearly a 70 percent rate. Burdick has established a culture of high expectations that would catch anyone's attention.

"It is pretty simple," he told me. "Students will always rise to the level of expectations you have of them. If I ask students to do homework, they will." But why do his students do the homework? We all ask students to do homework, and many of us don't have 50 percent pass rates or even 50 percent homework completion.

"We have to have a dialogue with students about homework," Burdick continued. "This is not a dictatorship; it is a democracy. If students have some ownership in the process of what we assign and when the work is due, they will have a better chance to complete it.

Once you establish that trust with students, this becomes part of the routine. Homework helps the students who complete it."

We must involve students in the process and design of our class.

I never would have used the "simplified and purposeful" method of assigning homework if it were not for my students. The spirit of design thinking is based on empathizing with the needs of our end users—our students. Homework was an essential part of my class, but it wasn't necessarily an essential part of my students' lives. We must ask our students to contribute to the class design. Once they are comfortable with this concept, teachers can also take this a step further and allow students to pick due dates, shift exams a day early or later, and even determine the assessments themselves. Design thinking helps us think differently—like Apple!

Remember, all of this is geared toward helping students who struggle. By taking an inventory about homework and other class policies, we engage students in the design process and help them own the collective work.

THE USE OF DATA

In education, the gap between the availability of data and the action surrounding it fascinates me. I remember spending an entire summer attempting to do an evaluation of a freshman mentoring program. We analyzed data on attendance, behavior, and grades, hoping to come to some conclusion as to whether the program was successful or not. The problem was that the data didn't tell the entire story. Too many other variables existed for us to conclude that the mentoring program was the reason for increased attendance or fewer failing grades. Simply put, we didn't have the right data.

Sometimes we have the data, but we cannot do anything about it! I worked with an intervention team of administrators at our school several years ago. We all wanted to find data to show the greater school community that we were responding to the trends we saw in our MTSS programming. We used tons of data—and even had an idea of what the data indicated—but due to restrictions within our contract, our current bell schedule, and other facility-related roadblocks, we couldn't initiate a response to some very glaring trends with our students.

Either way, it is fair to say that we can use data more effectively. The best teachers can use good data to help inform instructional decision-making. A principal could use data to communicate student progress to parents and the community. District administrators increasingly use data to help with resource allocation and the distribution of funds. And we all know the flip side of this: misuse of test scores can lead to labeling or stigmatization of our kids. Data without the context of students' background, socioeconomic status, and learning challenges contributes to misunderstanding groups of students. Even testing data can be taken too seriously, at the expense of other, more holistic outcomes we hope to see from our students.

A teacher who can effectively use data is dangerous, in a good way.

Jordan Dischinger-Smedes is one of those teachers who uses data dangerously. He teaches high school students in Grand Rapids, Michigan. Jordan deserves a lot of credit for the publication of this book, as he helped me recognize the need for a lifeline teachers can use to help struggling students. Jordan is passionate about tracking data and using it to inform his instruction. Jordan's system and commitment to data is more effective than mine, so we are lucky to have his voice and resources as a part of this book.

> **A TEACHER WHO CAN EFFECTIVELY USE DATA IS DANGEROUS, IN A GOOD WAY.**

I have learned a few things from Jordan. First, the power of data starts with showing the target. It is important that students see the standard and what it might look like. Some teachers like to put an advanced writing sample on the board and read it as a way for students to see what good writing looks like. Other teachers will show the work of a student on a math or science program to help students visualize the end goal. Even if students don't have context or skills yet, beginning with the end product in mind is a great strategy.

APES MCQ Grading Scale

AP Score	Credit Recommendation	College Grade Equivalent
5	Extremely well qualified	A
4	Well qualified	A-, B+, B
3	Qualified	B-, C+, C
2	Possibly qualified	n/a
1	No recommendation	n/a

2023 Average Raw MC% by Exam Score
1 → 42% (F, D-)
2 → 62% (D, D+, C-)
3 → 75% (C, C+, B-)
4 → 83 % (B, B+, A-)
5 → 91% (A)

MC Raw Score % (__/30)	Gradebook Score (%)
93 - 100 % (28, 29, 30)	97 - 100%
83 - 90% (25, 26, 27)	89 - 96%
73 - 80% (22, 23, 24)	79 - 86%
63 - 70% (19, 20, 21)	70 - 76%
53 - 60% (16, 17, 18)	64 - 68%
43 - 50 % (13, 14, 15)	59 - 62%
33 - 40 % (10, 11, 12)	56 - 58%
23 - 30 % (7, 8, 9)	53 - 55%
13 - 20% (4, 5, 6)	51 - 52%

The target goal of an AP Environmental Science class (APES) might be to pass the national exam. In this chart, students learn about their own class performance and what the correlation between their grade and their exam score might be.

Second, using data effectively with students involves self-reflection. John Hattie's meta-analysis shows a strong correlation between student reflection on their own performance and academic success. When students are given a chance to self-assess their work and set goals, they have a stronger chance of achievement. Hattie also argues that self-reported grades tend to affect student performance in positive ways. In this research, self-reported grades has an effective success rate of 1.33, which is far greater than the standard deviation of 0.4. In layman's terms, having students reflect on their grades has almost twice the impact on student performance as great techniques like classroom discussion, clear instruction, or reciprocal teaching.[8] Most students can honestly assess whether or not their work is aligned to the standards.

Environmental Science MCQ Unit Reflection Sheet		
Unit MCQ Test	Your Raw Test Score (3=75%, 4=83%, 5=91%)	Your reflection: Is this score where you want it to be based on your goal for our class? How prepared were you for this exam? Did you finish all your notes a few days before the test? Did you complete the review guide? What can you do on the next exam to be more prepared?
Ecosystem		
Biodiversity		
Populations		
Earth Systems		
Land Use		
Average Score:		

The document above shows a multiple-choice unit tracking sheet for an AP Environmental Science class. It gives students the opportunity to assess their progress toward a target score but also reflect on their own preparedness and performance.

Here are the questions asked of the students:

- Is this score what you want it to be based on your goals?
- How prepared were you for the exam?
- Did you have all your notes finished in advance of the exam?
- Did you complete the review guide?
- What can you do on the next exam to be more prepared?

Oftentimes, we look at data through the lens of how we can use it as teachers. This use of data and reflection allows students to use their own data to assess progress and growth. We spoke earlier about helping students believe that they can achieve something great and how we can convince our students of our belief in them. We are always convincing students of their greatness. Activities like these can help us along the way.

You may be familiar with author and researcher Carol Dweck and her work surrounding growth mindsets. I think the use of data pairs well with the concept that intelligence is not fixed but something we can continue to grow and foster. When we analyze data with students, we can help them identify their strengths and areas for growth. We can encourage them to reflect on their performance and consider what strategies or resources they can use to improve in areas where they may be struggling.[9] Hopefully, we can equip them with strategies to foster their growth. Moreover, I love the opportunity to build relationships in these conversations. Involving students in a conversation about their progress opens the door to building a relationship and helps them determine what they need most from their teacher.

"Data is the best way students can experience their own progress but also an alarm for students who struggle," remarked Janette Yao, who teaches in the New York City Public School system. "We use progress charts for students and let them enter their own grades. In this way, it becomes visual for students and creates a moment of reflection."

Allowing students to self-report grades is among John Hattie's recommended methods to increase student achievement, so not only is Yao engaging in an impactful instructional practice, she is also encouraging her students to take ownership of their own data.

At the same time, we want to build accountability through reflection and the positive use of data. When students search for answers as to why they may not grasp a certain topic or receive the grade they want, we can give them the tools to reflect on the progress they've made in their preparation. Reflection is not just about recognizing progress.

Reflection is also an opportunity to look in the mirror and ask, "Do I deserve it?"

Imagine handing a test back to a student with a poor grade on it. I always felt a little awkward in those moments. But when students have to reflect on why they received that grade, with these checklists, I believe the awkwardness would shift from the teacher to the student. We want to build this healthy reflection into our classes, knowing that when students recognize they can perform better, they will.

I remember handing back a unit test to one of my favorite students. It was the first failing grade he had ever received. I was dreading the walk back to his desk.

"Let's chat," I said as I handed him the exam.

He immediately broke eye contact with me to look at the exam, and I could tell he knew what was coming. He performed very well in the class, and this was a major surprise. What if I gave that student the opportunity to reflect on this before I graded the exam? The awkward moments would be eliminated. But moreover, he would have the opportunity to explain why this was a difficult concept or unit, or maybe that this was just a bad week in his life. These are valuable reflection points that help students grow.

In addition, both the teacher and the student will gain an understanding of the source of their struggle in an assessment. By targeting a specific standard, concept, or principle, we can find a solution for what might only be a deficiency in one area.

The core of differentiation begins with an in-depth analysis of student data. We can now formulate our plan of attack using different instructional methods, like small-group and homogeneous instruction. Teachers can also target instruction toward specific students or skills and deploy scaffolds for learning targeted to each individual student.

> ### *Ask the Author*
>
> **My student continues to struggle even after I've offered extensive support. I think they may need special education support or an IEP. Where do I begin?**
>
> We have to center all conversation on this topic around grade-level work. Standards exist for each grade level, and we should strive to meet and exceed them. When this is not the case, our job is not only to offer support, but to document and track its effectiveness. An IEP can be a powerful support, but often one that is misinterpreted and underutilized. An IEP is a last resort, used only when every general education intervention and tiered support has been exhausted. If teachers communicate effectively about progress and intervention attempts, the data collected will only help the IEP team find the best solution to support the student. I refer you back to the problem-solving process and list of supports provided earlier. Each school should have an exhaustive list of supports and programs, large and small, which can help students who struggle and target the source of these obstacles. How do we know that the student should be tested without the support and data on how well it worked?

Metacognition is defined as an awareness of one's own thought process. We want our students to activate this process and be able to evaluate their own thinking and performance. The more opportunities we give them to reflect, the more they take accountability for what they have done or—in many of our students' cases—have not done. In this way, we help create an ownership of learning. The more students put in, the more they get out. Though these examples are from high school, I believe this concept is somewhat universal. Even if you teach kindergarten, there is great value in asking students if they practiced their sight words or math flash cards.

Not all data analysis and reflection needs to be predictable or this formal. In fact, I think there is a lot of power in asking students unanticipated questions. I find myself constantly answering unanticipated questions from colleagues. They keep me on my toes and make me reflect on my own thinking and decision-making. So, what if we asked students "why" more often? What if we asked students how they arrived at a certain answer or encouraged students to read their own writing out loud? What if we took advantage of those informal moments to drive home the importance of "thinking about their thinking"?

We have to make time for students to reflect on their data. Jordan's commitment to student reflection is a call to action for all of us. While we may not have an existing system that allows for reflection at this level, we have to start building time for this in our class. Data without an action plan is a waste.

The action plan can be as simple as this checklist:

- Create a goal and show students how to achieve it. Write it down.
- Allow for students to track their progress in the short and long term.
- Compare student data to show growth longitudinally.
- Convince students to reflect on their preparedness as a prediction of their performance.

CHAPTER SUMMARY

Beliefs about assessment, homework, and data are individual and can be emotional for many teachers. They reflect the academic culture of our class. While it may be hard to rethink these important staples, I urge you to explore all three categories with an open mind. Students who struggle can benefit from reinforcement of content, and the idea of preventing learning plateaus is one strategy to help them hold their thinking. Half of each assessment should include questions from previous assessments. Genuine reflection on the value of homework is also critical. If homework is necessary, teachers should only assign one thing for homework with regularity and consistency throughout the year. Students will then see the value and purpose behind it. Finally, teachers who have data are good. Teachers who use data are powerful. We must learn to use data to create opportunities for students to reflect on their progress and to help them create long- and short-term goals for the rest of the course. While this may not reflect the most personal chapter of the book, these classroom policies and methods represent the foundation of how a teacher's class functions.

EPILOGUE

My heartfelt hope is that you will feel motivated and inspired by what you have just read. Everyone who invests time in a book like this should take away practical ideas that are usable in class tomorrow, and I hope I've delivered. I've tried to include as many stories from teachers who, like you, are doing amazing work daily. In obtaining these stories, I found kindred spirits and a connection with these teachers, knowing that we are facing these same challenges together. We should acknowledge the difficulty of our jobs, since many folks outside our profession just don't seem to get it.

Teaching is a noble profession, and society is counting on us. We've committed to a lifelong goal of helping kids achieve academic and personal success. Part of this calling is to help our students shift their focus from achievement to growth. If we value this in all we say and do with students, their attention will turn toward their own progress instead of the standards by which students seem to be judged. This is a worthwhile endeavor, one that will leave you satisfied as you watch your students reshape their opinion of themselves. Through self-assessment, students will begin to know themselves better, which can only help them in school and in many other facets of life.

Lately, it too often seems as if people in our society have become obsessed with changing the world by making everyone else change. Teachers have often been the target of this, as folks outside of education try to influence how and what students should be taught. We recognize these people at work too, who believe we should all have to adjust to the way they are instead of expecting them to look in the mirror to assess how they can improve. We can also be guilty of this when we blame administration, parents, or the community for the struggles our students experience, thus making our jobs more difficult.

Each one of us plays an important role in our school, district, community, society, and world. We all have a profound effect on our friends and family. That is a given.

The calling for us, as professionals, is how we affect ordinary people, namely, our students.

If we want to change the world, we should start by changing ourselves. Greg Harden, a life coach who has worked with celebrities from Tom Brady to Michael Phelps, says, "A human being is the only person who can decide to be something different tomorrow. A zebra will be a zebra. A dog will be a dog. A bird will be a bird. But you can wake up tomorrow, look in the mirror, and say, 'I want to be a different person, and a better person.'"[1]

We are amazing teachers, and we all can still improve. Both things can be true. We can reflect and deliberately make changes so our lives and careers can be more fulfilling. In doing so, we will affect the lives of countless others and contribute positively to a better world. If that sounds idealistic, it is. How many other professions can boast this type of impact?

I am a work in progress, someone who struggles daily to live up to the ideals and principles I write about. Join me in this struggle and this challenge, because there are students now—and in the future—who are counting on us.

Book Study Cheat Sheet

I thought hard about whether or not to include this section. I did not want to give readers an easy out by including this cheat sheet. If you cracked open this section of the book, promise me that you reread the assigned chapters. The impactful stories and advice from teachers around the country hopefully make some of these strategies come alive. But if you have not yet read what you were supposed to, I've been there. In fact, that was most of college for me!

I understand and I empathize. If you've stumbled on this section and you did read the entire book, you are in good hands too. May this serve as your study guide and your safety net in conversations with your colleagues.

CHAPTER 1: BUILDING CULTURE

- Evaluate the culture of the class using a survey or template. Begin to be more intentional about favoring culture over content and skills. Most teachers are amazing with their content and how to teach it. The teachers who focus on culture first are the best teachers I've seen.
- Commit to the effort it takes to sustain culture. A school year is long, and a teaching career is longer. Culture can change over time, and so the teacher must adapt. There are parts of a classroom culture that no longer work or are ineffective. Be willing to change and create something bigger and better!

- Relationships and culture are very closely related. Whole-class and individual relationships are different but are equally important in driving the success of the class.

CHAPTER 2: MOTIVATION

- Students struggle for a variety of reasons. Understanding the motivation or lack thereof with students is paramount in understanding the behavior. Seek the root causes of struggle in order to find the solutions to motivate the student.
- Modeling for students is a powerful tool. If you want something done right, show them the pathway and an example of what it should look like. Students who struggle may have never seen a powerful example of academic work. We can provide this.
- Create goals for students. Oftentimes, we ask students, "What is your goal?" We should be ahead of this question—driving the conversation around short- and long-term goals for their school year and beyond.
- Commit to an "IEP-type" of pathway for all kids. Each student needs an individual plan for success. As you seek ways to motivate the masses, know and understand that each student needs to be taught and coached differently, and should be.

CHAPTER 3: ATTACKING SKILL DEFICIENCY

- Students are not reading unless they have a pen in their hand. Reading and literacy are important in all of our classes. We are all reading teachers. Students cannot do this effectively unless we assign specific tasks to accompany the readings. We must consistently ask ourselves, "What are the students doing while they are reading?"
- Great culture is derived from habits. What habits do you want students to form as they progress through the school year?

Academic habits can range from organization, preparedness, and in-class behaviors. Model these for students so they can visualize the expectations we have for them.

- Many of our students are willing to study and review, but they do not know how. We can spend our valuable class time to teach them how and increase the number of tools in their toolbox to prepare and review for a large assessment.

CHAPTER 4: BE THE DIFFERENCE

- Students should look up to you as a role model and example. You are the leader of the class, and the students will draft off your behaviors and the attitudes you project. Choose and model these wisely.
- Many of our students have never been told that they can do it. Intentionally instill confidence in students with the knowledge that you may be the only one who believes in them. This interaction will pay dividends in establishing a trusting relationship with kids.
- Be mindful of the inequities that exist in the groups of students in your class. Redouble your effort with the students who struggle most, knowing that each student in the class—like each player on the team—needs something different from you. Understand that one of the groups that struggles the most are our boys. Think about what the data shows and how you can develop a strategy for helping those who need it most.

CHAPTER 5: ASSESSMENT, HOMEWORK, AND DATA

- Consider assessing students cumulatively. We never want students to lose the knowledge and skills they gained throughout the year. Each exam or assessment should include review questions to help with retention.

- Homework should be simplified at all costs. It plays a very precarious role in the lives of our students outside of class. If you choose to assign homework, find the one task that is irreplaceable and foundational to success in your class, and have students complete that—and only that. We only should assign one thing all year for homework completion.
- Consider ways for students to reflect on their own progress. Self-evaluation is one of the most impactful tools for students to use. Give students an opportunity to track and celebrate progress.

Book Study Questions

CHAPTER 1: BUILDING CULTURE

- What strategies or activities from your own culture inventory can you share with the group? What are you proud of? What do students internalize?
- Are you convinced that culture can help struggling students? Why or why not?
- Do you believe culture has nothing to do with personality but everything to do with a teacher's willingness to create a unique and different experience for kids?
- What role does culture play in helping kids gain more skills and learn more content?
- Which of the ten ideas presented in chapter 1 can you commit to? What might this look like in your class?

CHAPTER 2: MOTIVATION

- What strategies do you use to motivate students who lack motivation? How does this differ from individual students to the entire class?
- How have you worked to find root causes of motivation with individual students, and has that helped them make more academic and personal progress?
- In what ways do you create goals for students, and in what ways are students allowed to create goals for themselves?

- Give an example of how you have created an individual pathway for a student toward a goal. How can you scale this exercise to creating motivation and targeted goals for the entire class?

CHAPTER 3: ATTACKING SKILL DEFICIENCY

- When a student cannot comprehend a text, what is your favorite and best strategy to help him/her?
- When you are about to assign a difficult reading to the entire class, how do you help them before, during, and after they read?
- Of the resources shared, which can be readily made into a lesson in your class, and what content would you use?
- How do you teach study skills and organization skills to students currently? Which strategy shared in this chapter would add to your toolbox?

CHAPTER 4: BE THE DIFFERENCE

- How do you make individual students more confident in themselves? How do you instill confidence among the entire class?
- Which strategies presented in this book may be successful with your students? Why?
- Which group of students deserves more of your attention? What do you plan to do, change, or initiate, and why?
- In what ways will you differentiate individual relationships with whole-class relationships?

CHAPTER 5: ASSESSMENT, HOMEWORK, AND DATA

- How are students in your class held accountable for previously learned material?

- What percentage of your unit exams or large assignments include review questions, and is there room for more of this style of assessment?
- What is your current homework policy? How can you adapt or adopt Andrew's simple and purposeful homework beliefs?
- Do students have a voice in the design of your class policies? How do you plan to incorporate more student voices in this design?
- How do you use data to inform your instruction?
- How do students use data about their own performance to help guide and inform their learning?

Acknowledgments

It took me so long to put this together! I've written two books before, but at different times of my life with fewer distractions, competing priorities, and personal challenges. Sharing my passion for helping kids in this book has been such a blessing, one that could have never happened without the help of so many people.

First, "the house don't fall when the bones are good." To my wife and best friend, Lizzie, and our three boys, Cooper, Parker, and Beckett: thank you always for supporting Dad's work. You bear the burden of my schedule—late nights at school, many days on the road, seemingly each moment of the day accounted for; you greet me at the door with a smile and hug regardless. It allows me to push forward and live an amazing life with you. There is nothing the five of us cannot do together. I love you.

To my parents, David and Ingrid, and my sister, Nicole, thank you for your unending support. I know my priorities and my calendar prevent me from being the son and brother you probably deserve, but I love you and value the time we spend together. I won the family lottery!

I am so thankful to have found a publisher who is willing to share this message. To Dave, Tara, Wendy, Lindsey, Dana, and the entire team: I owe you this portion of my career. I cannot tell you how much I enjoy working with you, and I hope the feeling is mutual. I am a DBC Pirate for life.

I feel completely humbled reading the foreword to this book. Brian worked very hard on this and it shows. Brian—thank you for everything you have taught me and for your friendship. You've shaped who I am as a teacher, coach, father, husband, and man. I love you, man.

To Leyden High School, the Board of Education, and Superintendent Dr. Nick Polyak, I am humbled at the support you've given me in every role I've had in our district. Thank you for taking a chance on me, multiple times. I still have fifteen years left to try and pay it off. ☺

To all those who partner with me for professional development, allowing me the privilege to work with your faculty and staff, it has been an absolute honor. I have learned more from you and your staff than I could ever imagine. Our PD sessions and collaboration together completes me.

To my former, current, and future players, we've only just begun. I am proud of you and will always be your coach. Whatever it takes . . . together.

And finally, to my former students—thank you for running through a wall for me. I am proud that your accomplishments will inspire others for years to come. Know that I will be forever in your corner and will help you however I can.

About the Author

Andrew Sharos has proudly spent his entire teaching career at Leyden High School District 212 in suburban Chicago. He earned his undergraduate degree from Marquette University, his master's from Olivet Nazarene University, and his endorsement in School Business from Northern Illinois University.

Andrew has been a teacher, coach, assistant principal, and district administrator—still working at Leyden High School where it all began. He is the founder and CEO of the Village Project Consulting Group, which provides professional development to schools to improve their instructional outcomes and their overall building culture. Andrew offers professional development centered around instructional methods, culture-building, training new teachers, creating high expectations, leadership coaching, and infusing literacy effectively into the classroom. He has keynoted and presented at conferences across the country.

Andrew's first book, *All 4s and 5s: A Guide to Teaching and Leading Advanced Placement Programs*, has become the best-selling book in the AP community. The book has been used by entire faculties for professional development and book studies. Andrew's second book, with Andrew Grieve, *Finding Lifelines: A Practical Tale About Teachers and Mentors*, has become a go-to guide for new teachers at all levels. This book also is available as an online course, which many districts have adopted for new teacher training. Andrew has also authored two manuals with the Bureau of Education and Research, both focused on using technology and flipped classroom methods in social studies.

He can be found on X at @AndrewSharosAP, online at AndrewSharos.com, or through email at andrew.sharos@gmail.com. Andrew has been married to his wife, Lizzie, since 2009. Andrew and Lizzie live in suburban Chicago with their three sons, Cooper, Parker, and Beckett. Andrew spends his free time coaching their sports teams and planning their next family vacation.

Want Andrew to partner with your staff or leadership team? Scan the QR code to learn more about professional development, workshops, or keynotes with Andrew.

Endnotes

INTRODUCTION

1. John Hattie, *Visible Learning + Visible Learning for Teachers* (Corwin, 2014).
2. National Center for Education Statistics. 2017. "Back-to-School Statistics." Nces.ed.gov. December 31, 2017. https://nces.ed.gov/fastfacts/display.asp?id=372.

CHAPTER 1

1. Ryan Hawk, *The Learning Leader Show*, episode 467, "Marcus Buckingham: How to Find Love in Your Work, Designing the Future of Education, and Breaking All the Rules," April 10, 2022.
2. Liz Mineo, "Good Genes Are Nice, but Joy Is Better." *Harvard Gazette*. April 11, 2017. https://news.harvard.edu/gazette/story/2017/04/over-nearly-80-years-harvard-study-has-been-showing-how-to-live-a-healthy-and-happy-life/.
3. Ryan Hawk, *The Learning Leader Show*, episode 461, "Brad Meltzer: How to Tell Your Story, Respond from Rejection, and Love Your Work," February 27, 2022.

CHAPTER 2

1. Kevin Eastman, *Why the Best Are the Best: 25 Powerful Words That Impact, Inspire, and Define Champions* (Advantage, 2018).
2. Alexandre Sokolowski, "May 5, 2005: The Day Andy Roddick's Sportsmanship Cost Him a Win," *Tennis Majors*, May 5, 2024. https://www.tennismajors.com/our-features/on-this-day/may-5-2005-the-day-andy-roddicks-sportsmanship-cost-him-victory-210307.html.
3. Francis Storrs, "Dunkin's Run: A Love Story," *Boston* magazine, August 30, 2010, https://www.bostonmagazine.com/2010/08/30/dunkins-run-a-love-story/.

CHAPTER 3

1. "'Don't Let Schooling Interfere with Your Education'- Mark Twain." n.d. Vanderbilt University. https://admissions.vanderbilt.edu/insidedores/2013/12/dont-let-schooling-interfere-with-your-education-mark-twain/.
2. Michael Manderino, Roberta L. Berglund, and Jerry L. Johns, *Content Area Learning: Bridges to Disciplinary Literacy* (Kendall Hunt, 2014).

3   Zaretta L. Hammond, *Culturally Responsive Teaching and the Brain* (SAGE Publications, 2015).

4   Joe Feldman. *Grading for Equity* (Corwin, 2018).

5   "Harvard's Arthur C. Brooks on the Secrets to Happiness at Work," *Harvard Business Review*, September 1, 2023, https://hbr.org/2023/09/harvards-arthur-c-brooks-on-the-secrets-to-happiness-at-work.

CHAPTER 4

1   "Brian Kight" (blog), Tbriankight.com, July 2023.

2   Sungju Lee and Susan Elizabeth McClelland, *Every Falling Star* (Abrams, 2016).

3   Ben Johnson, "Working to Grow Students' Trust and Respect," *Edutopia*, October 10, 2018, https://www.edutopia.org/article/working-grow-students-trust-and-respect/.

4   Melissa S. Kearney and Phillip B. Levine, "Role Models, Mentors, and Media Influences," *The Future of Children* 30 (2020): 83–106, https://doi.org/10.1353/foc.2020.0006.

5   Katie Nodjimbadem, "The Trashy Beginnings of 'Don't Mess with Texas,'" *Smithsonian* magazine, March 10, 2017, https://www.smithsonianmag.com/history/trashy-beginnings-dont-mess-texas-180962490/.

6   "YouTube Advice from MrBeast (26 Million Subscribers)." Cutback.video. 2025. https://cutback.video/blog/mrbeast-youtube-advise-ko.

7   Ryan Hawk, *The Learning Leader Show*, episode 528, "Seth Godin: A New Manifesto for Teams: Innovation, Creativity, Hiring, Firing, and the Power of Speed (The Song of Significance)," May 22, 2023.

8   Tesfaye Nigussie, "The Effect of Time Management Practice on the Academic Achievement: A Case of Dire Dawa University, Ethiopia," *European Journal of Business and Management* 11, no. 4 (2019). https://doi.org/10.7176/ejbm/11-4-05.

9   Eric Potterat and Alan Eagle, *Learned Excellence* (HarperCollins, 2024).

10 Cathy Vatterott, *Rethinking Grading* (ASCD, 2015).

11 National Center for Education Statistics. "Public High School Graduation Rates." Nces.ed.gov. National Center for Education Statistics. May 2021. https://nces.ed.gov/programs/coe/indicator/coi/high-school-graduation-rates.

12 John H. Clarke, *Personalized Learning: Student-Designed Pathways to High School Graduation* (Corwin, 2013).

13 Richard V. Reeves, *Of Boys and Men* (Brookings Institution Press, 2022).

14 Steven J. Stanton and Oliver C. Schultheiss, "The Hormonal Correlates of Implicit Power Motivation," *Journal of Research in Personality* 43, no. 5 (2009): 942–949, https://doi.org/10.1016/j.jrp.2009.04.001.

15. Franchesca Cortes, "'Colorblindness' and White Privilege," *Adolescent Learners in Urban Contexts* (blog), December 11, 2018. https://wp.nyu.edu/urbanyouthnyu/2018/12/11/colorblindness-as-a-privilege/.

CHAPTER 5

1. Elizabeth Ligon Bjork and Robert A. Bjork. *Memory.* Academic Press, 1996.
2. Nicholas J. Cepeda, Edward Vul, Doug Rohrer, John T. Wixted, and Harold Pashler, "Spacing Effects in Learning: A Temporal Ridgeline of Optimal Retention," *Psychological Science* 19, no. 11 (2008): 1095–1102, https://doi.org/10.1111/j.1467-9280.2008.02209.x.
3. Doug Rohrer and Kelli Taylor, "The Shuffling of Mathematics Problems Improves Learning," *Instructional Science* 35, no. 6 (2007): 481–498, https://doi.org/10.1007/s11251-007-9015-8.
4. Harris Cooper, Jorgianne Civey Robinson, and Erika A. Patall, "Does Homework Improve Academic Achievement? A Synthesis of Research, 1987–2003," *Review of Educational Research* 76, no. 1 (2006): 1–62, https://doi.org/10.3102/00346543076001001.
5. Zameena Mejia, "How a Cold Call Helped a Young Steve Jobs Score His First Internship at Hewlett-Packard," CNBC, July 26, 2018, https://www.cnbc.com/2018/07/25/how-steve-jobs-cold-called-his-way-to-an-internship-at-hewlett-packard.html
6. Zameena Mejia, "How a Cold Call Helped a Young Steve Jobs Score His First Internship at Hewlett-Packard," CNBC, July 26, 2018, https://www.cnbc.com/2018/07/25/how-steve-jobs-cold-called-his-way-to-an-internship-at-hewlett-packard.html.
7. Joshua Angrist and Victor Lavy, "The Effects of High Stakes High School Achievement Awards: Evidence from a Randomized Trial," *American Economic Review* 99, no. 4 (2009): 1384–1414, https://doi.org/10.1257/aer.99.4.1384.
8. John Hattie, *Visible Learning for Teachers* (Corwin, 2014).
9. Carol S. Dweck, *Mindset: The New Psychology of Success* (Random House, 2006).

EPILOGUE

1. Ryan Hawk, *The Learning Leader Show*, episode 551, "Greg Harden: How to Control the Controllables and Stay Sane in an Insane World (A Conversation with Tom Brady's Mentor)," November 2, 2023.

Since 2012, DBCI has published books that inspire and equip educators to be their best. For more information on our titles or to purchase bulk orders for your school, district, or book study, visit DaveBurgessConsulting.com/DBCIbooks.

THE *LIKE A PIRATE*™ SERIES

Teach Like a PIRATE by Dave Burgess
eXPlore Like a PIRATE by Michael Matera
Learn Like a PIRATE by Paul Solarz
Plan Like a PIRATE by Dawn M. Harris
Play Like a PIRATE by Quinn Rollins
Run Like a PIRATE by Adam Welcome
Tech Like a PIRATE by Matt Miller

THE *LEAD LIKE A PIRATE*™ SERIES

Lead Like a PIRATE by Shelley Burgess and Beth Houf
Balance Like a PIRATE by Jessica Cabeen, Jessica Johnson, and Sarah Johnson
Lead beyond Your Title by Nili Bartley
Lead with Appreciation by Amber Teamann and Melinda Miller
Lead with Collaboration by Allyson Apsey and Jessica Gomez
Lead with Culture by Jay Billy
Lead with Instructional Rounds by Vicki Wilson
Lead with Literacy by Mandy Ellis
She Leads by Dr. Rachael George and Majalise W. Tolan

THE EDUPROTOCOL FIELD GUIDE SERIES

Deploying EduProtocols by Kim Voge, with Jon Corippo and Marlena Hebern

The EduProtocol Field Guide by Marlena Hebern and Jon Corippo

The EduProtocol Field Guide Book 2 by Marlena Hebern and Jon Corippo

The EduProtocol Field Guide Math Edition by Lisa Nowakowski and Jeremiah Ruesch

The EduProtocol Field Guide Primary Edition by Benjamin Cogswell and Jennifer Dean

The EduProtocol Field Guide Social Studies Edition by Dr. Scott M. Petri and Adam Moler

The EduProtocol Field Guide ELA Edition by Jacob Carr

LEADERSHIP & SCHOOL CULTURE

Be 1% Better by Ron Clark

Be THAT Teacher by Dwayne Reed

Beyond the Surface of Restorative Practices by Marisol Rerucha

Change the Narrative by Henry J. Turner and Kathy Lopes

Choosing to See by Pamela Seda and Kyndall Brown

Culturize by Jimmy Casas

Discipline Win by Andy Jacks

Educate Me! by Dr. Shree Walker with Micheal D. Ison

Escaping the School Leader's Dunk Tank by Rebecca Coda and Rick Jetter

Fight Song by Kim Bearden

From Teacher to Leader by Starr Sackstein

If the Dance Floor Is Empty, Change the Song by Joe Clark

The Innovator's Mindset by George Couros

It's OK to Say "They" by Christy Whittlesey

Kids Deserve It! by Todd Nesloney and Adam Welcome

Leading the Whole Teacher by Allyson Apsey

Let Them Speak by Rebecca Coda and Rick Jetter

The Limitless School by Abe Hege and Adam Dovico

Live Your Excellence by Jimmy Casas

Next-Level Teaching by Jonathan Alsheimer

The Pepper Effect by Sean Gaillard

Principaled by Kate Barker, Kourtney Ferrua, and Rachael George
The Principled Principal by Jeffrey Zoul and Anthony McConnell
Relentless by Hamish Brewer
The Secret Solution by Todd Whitaker, Sam Miller, and Ryan Donlan
Start. Right. Now. by Todd Whitaker, Jeffrey Zoul, and Jimmy Casas
Stop. Right. Now. by Jimmy Casas and Jeffrey Zoul
Teach Your Class Off by CJ Reynolds
Teachers Deserve It by Rae Hughart and Adam Welcome
They Call Me "Mr. De" by Frank DeAngelis
Thrive through the Five by Jill M. Siler
Unmapped Potential by Julie Hasson and Missy Lennard
When Kids Lead by Todd Nesloney and Adam Dovico
Word Shift by Joy Kirr
Your School Rocks by Ryan McLane and Eric Lowe

TECHNOLOGY & TOOLS

50 Things to Go Further with Google Classroom by Alice Keeler and Libbi Miller
50 Things You Can Do with Google Classroom by Alice Keeler and Libbi Miller
50 Ways to Engage Students with Google Apps by Alice Keeler and Heather Lyon
140 Twitter Tips for Educators by Brad Currie, Billy Krakower, and Scott Rocco
Block Breaker by Brian Aspinall
Building Blocks for Tiny Techies by Jamila "Mia" Leonard
Code Breaker by Brian Aspinall
The Complete EdTech Coach by Katherine Goyette and Adam Juarez
Control Alt Achieve by Eric Curts
The Esports Education Playbook by Chris Aviles, Steve Isaacs, Christine Lion-Bailey, and Jesse Lubinsky
Google Apps for Littles by Christine Pinto and Alice Keeler
Master the Media by Julie Smith
Raising Digital Leaders by Jennifer Casa-Todd
Reality Bytes by Christine Lion-Bailey, Jesse Lubinsky, and Micah Shippee, PhD

Sail the 7 Cs with Microsoft Education by Becky Keene and Kathi Kersznowski
Shake Up Learning by Kasey Bell
Social LEADia by Jennifer Casa-Todd
Stepping Up to Google Classroom by Alice Keeler and Kimberly Mattina
Teaching Math with Google Apps by Alice Keeler and Diana Herrington
Teaching with Google Jamboard by Alice Keeler and Kimberly Mattina
Teachingland by Amanda Fox and Mary Ellen Weeks

TEACHING METHODS & MATERIALS

All 4s and 5s by Andrew Sharos
Boredom Busters by Katie Powell
Building Strong Writers by Christina Schneider
The Classroom Chef by John Stevens and Matt Vaudrey
The Collaborative Classroom by Trevor Muir
Copyrighteous by Diana Gill
CREATE by Bethany J. Petty
Ditch That Homework by Matt Miller and Alice Keeler
Ditch That Textbook by Matt Miller
Don't Ditch That Tech by Matt Miller, Nate Ridgway, and Angelia Ridgway
EDrenaline Rush by John Meehan
Educated by Design by Michael Cohen, The Tech Rabbi
Empowered to Choose: A Practical Guide to Personalized Learning by Andrew Easton
Expedition Science by Becky Schnekser
Frustration Busters by Katie Powell
Fully Engaged by Michael Matera and John Meehan
Game On? Brain On! by Lindsay Portnoy, PhD
Guided Math AMPED by Reagan Tunstall
Happy & Resilient by Roni Habib
Innovating Play by Jessica LaBar-Twomy and Christine Pinto
Instant Relevance by Denis Sheeran
Instructional Coaching Connection by Nathan Lang-Raad
Keeping the Wonder by Jenna Copper, Ashley Bible, Abby Gross, and Staci Lamb

LAUNCH by John Spencer and A.J. Juliani
Learning in the Zone by Dr. Sonny Magana
Lights, Cameras, TEACH! by Kevin J. Butler
Make Learning MAGICAL by Tisha Richmond
Pass the Baton by Kathryn Finch and Theresa Hoover
Project-Based Learning Anywhere by Lori Elliott
Pure Genius by Don Wettrick
The Revolution by Darren Ellwein and Derek McCoy
The Science Box by Kim Adsit and Adam Peterson
Shift This! by Joy Kirr
Skyrocket Your Teacher Coaching by Michael Cary Sonbert
Spark Learning by Ramsey Musallam
Sparks in the Dark by Travis Crowder and Todd Nesloney
Table Talk Math by John Stevens
Teachables by Cheryl Abla and Lisa Maxfield
Unpack Your Impact by Naomi O'Brien and LaNesha Tabb
The Wild Card by Hope and Wade King
Writefully Empowered by Jacob Chastain
The Writing on the Classroom Wall by Steve Wyborney
You Are Poetry by Mike Johnston
You'll Never Guess What I'm Saying by Naomi O'Brien
You'll Never Guess What I'm Thinking About by Naomi O'Brien

INSPIRATION, PROFESSIONAL GROWTH & PERSONAL DEVELOPMENT

Be REAL by Tara Martin
Be the One for Kids by Ryan Sheehy
The Coach ADVenture by Amy Illingworth
Creatively Productive by Lisa Johnson
The Ed Branding Book by Dr. Renae Bryant and Lynette White
Educational Eye Exam by Alicia Ray
The EduNinja Mindset by Jennifer Burdis
Empower Our Girls by Lynmara Colón and Adam Welcome
Finding Lifelines by Andrew Grieve and Andrew Sharos
The Four O'Clock Faculty by Rich Czyz
How Much Water Do We Have? by Pete and Kris Nunweiler

P Is for Pirate by Dave and Shelley Burgess
A Passion for Kindness by Tamara Letter
The Path to Serendipity by Allyson Apsey
PheMOMenal Teacher by Annick Rauch
Recipes for Resilience by Robert A. Martinez
Rogue Leader by Rich Czyz
Sanctuaries by Dan Tricarico
Saving Sycamore by Molly B. Hudgens
The Secret Sauce by Rich Czyz
Shattering the Perfect Teacher Myth by Aaron Hogan
Stories from Webb by Todd Nesloney
Talk to Me by Kim Bearden
Teach Better by Chad Ostrowski, Tiffany Ott, Rae Hughart, and Jeff Gargas
Teach Me, Teacher by Jacob Chastain
Teach, Play, Learn! by Adam Peterson
Teaching Is a Tattoo by Mike Johnston
The Teachers of Oz by Herbie Raad and Nathan Lang-Raad
Teaching the Ms. Abbott Way by Joyce Stephens Abbott
TeamMakers by Laura Robb and Evan Robb
Through the Lens of Serendipity by Allyson Apsey
Write Here and Now by Dan Tricarico
The Zen Teacher by Dan Tricarico

CHILDREN'S BOOKS

The Adventures of Little Mickey by Mickey Smith Jr.
Alpert by LaNesha Tabb
Alpert & Friends by LaNesha Tabb
Beyond Us by Aaron Polansky
Cannonball In by Tara Martin
Dolphins in Trees by Aaron Polansky
Dragon Smart by Tisha and Tommy Richmond
I Can Achieve Anything by MoNique Waters
I Want to Be a Lot by Ashley Savage
The Magic of Wonder by Jenna Copper, Ashley Bible, Abby Gross, and Staci Lamb

Micah's Big Question by Naomi O'Brien

The Princes of Serendip by Allyson Apsey

Ride with Emilio by Richard Nares

A Teacher's Top Secret Confidential by LaNesha Tabb

A Teacher's Top Secret: Mission Accomplished by LaNesha Tabb

The Wild Card Kids by Hope and Wade King

Zom-Be a Design Thinker by Amanda Fox

www.ingramcontent.com/pod-product-compliance
Lightning Source LLC
Chambersburg PA
CBHW050527170426

43201CB00013B/2120